# Saving Seeds Handbook

A Seed Saving Guide for Gardeners to Sow, Harvest, Clean, and Store Vegetable and Flower Seeds Plus Techniques To Get You Started

By

Zera Brooks

# Copyright © 2022 – Zera Brooks

## All rights reserved

No part of this publication may be reproduced, distributed, or transmitted in any form or by any means, including photocopying, recording, or other electronic or mechanical methods, without the prior written permission of the publisher, except in the case of brief quotations embodied in reviews and certain other non-commercial uses permitted by copyright law.

## Disclaimer

This publication is designed to provide competent and reliable information regarding the subject matter covered. However, the views expressed in this publication are those of the author alone, and should not be taken as expert instruction or professional advice. The reader is responsible for his or her own actions.

The author hereby disclaims any responsibility or liability whatsoever that is incurred from the use or application of the contents of this publication by the purchaser or reader. The purchaser or reader is hereby responsible for his or her own actions.

# Table of Contents

Introduction ................................................................... 8

Chapter 1 ..................................................................... 10

The Basics of Saving Seeds ........................................ 10

    What is a Seed? ..................................................... 10

    Types of Seeds ....................................................... 11

    Anatomy of Seed ................................................... 13

    How Are Seeds Formed? ...................................... 17

    Saving Seeds Terminology .................................. 18

    Why Save Seeds? ................................................... 25

Chapter 2 ..................................................................... 29

Planning For Seed Production .................................. 29

    Choosing Seeds for Saving ................................. 29

    Plant Life-Cycles ................................................... 31

    Planning Your Population Size .......................... 32

    Isolation of Varieties ............................................ 36

- By Distance.................................................................. 38
- By Barrier..................................................................... 40
- Bagging ....................................................................... 40
- Caging ........................................................................ 41
- By Time ....................................................................... 42
- Hand Pollination .............................................................. 42

Growing Seeds – Indoor or Outdoor ................................. 47

- Indoor Seed Planting ...................................................... 47
- Outdoor Seed Planting ................................................... 52
- Seeds to Plant Indoor or Outdoor .................................... 55

Chapter 3 ........................................................................ 61

Harvesting Mature Seeds................................................. 61

Harvesting Guidelines ..................................................... 61

Supply List for Harvesting Seeds ..................................... 62

Timing The Harvest.......................................................... 63

- Dry Seeded Crops .......................................................... 66
- Wet Seeded Crops ......................................................... 68

Processing The Seeds...................................................... 70

- Processing Dry Seeds..................................................... 70
- Processing Wet Seeds .................................................... 73

Final Drying of Seeds for Storage .................................... 77

Factors Affecting Seed Storage Longevity...................... 79

Labeling ............................................................................... 84
Testing Seed Quality ........................................................... 85

Chapter 4 ................................................................................ 93

Saving Vegetable Seeds ........................................................ 93

Common Vegetable Family To Save Seeds From .............. 93

Solanaceae: Tobacco or Nightshade Family ................... 93
Fabaceae (Leguminosae): Bean or Pea Family ............... 94
Cucurbitaceae: Gourd Family ........................................... 95
Malvaceae: Mallow or Hibiscus Family .......................... 96
Alliaceae, Liliaceae or Amaryillidaceae: Onion Family 97
Poaceae (Gramineae): Grasses or Grains Family ........... 98
Brassicaceae (Cruciferae): Mustard Family .................... 99
Chenopodiaceae: Goosefoot Family .............................. 100
Amaranthaceae: Pigweed Or Amaranth Family ......... 101
Apiaceae (Umbelliferae): Parsley Family ..................... 101
Lamiaceae (Labiatae): Mint Family ............................... 102

Saving Seeds Quick Guide of Common Vegetables ....... 103

Beans ................................................................................... 104
Beets .................................................................................... 104
Broccoli ............................................................................... 105
Brussel Sprouts ................................................................. 105
Cabbage .............................................................................. 105
Carrot .................................................................................. 106
Cauliflower ........................................................................ 106
Corn ..................................................................................... 107

  Cucumbers ............................................................. 107
  Eggplant ................................................................ 108
  Lettuce .................................................................. 108
  Melon .................................................................... 108
  Okra ...................................................................... 109
  Onions .................................................................. 109
  Peas ...................................................................... 109
  Peppers ................................................................ 110
  Pumpkins ............................................................ 110
  Radish .................................................................. 110
  Spinach ................................................................ 111
  Squash .................................................................. 111
  Tomatoes ............................................................. 111
Chapter 5 ....................................................................... 112

Saving Flower Seeds ................................................... 112

 Saving Seeds From Common Flowers ............................. 112

  Calendula ............................................................ 113
  Zinnia ................................................................... 116
  Cosmos ................................................................ 121
  Morning Glory ................................................... 125
  Nasturtium ......................................................... 129
  Sunflower ............................................................ 134
  Marigold ............................................................. 138
  Sweet Pea ............................................................ 142
  Lupine .................................................................. 147
  California Poppy ................................................ 152

Chapter 6 ................................................................................. 160

Seed Saving Mistakes To Avoid ............................................ 160

Conclusion ............................................................................. 166

# Introduction

In gardening and agriculture, seed saving (also known as brown-bagging) is the process of saving seeds from vegetables, herbs, grains, and flowers for use year after year. For the past 12,000 years, this has been the conventional method of maintaining farms and gardens. There has been a substantial change in recent times, beginning in the latter half of the twentieth century to acquiring seed yearly from commercial seed providers. It is on record that home gardeners are responsible for a large portion of today's grassroots seed-saving activity.

To thrive at seed saving, you need to learn new skills to ensure that essential characteristics are preserved in the plant variety's landraces. The minimum distance between plants of similar species is required to prevent cross-pollination with another variety, as well as the minimum number of plants that need to be grown to preserve innate genetic diversity, are both important considerations gardeners need to pay attention to. It's also important to identify the cultivar's ideal characteristics so that when grown, plants that aren't breeding "true" are picked against. Seed-borne diseases must also be identified so that they can be eradicated. Seed storage procedures must be effective enough to keep the seed viable. It's important to know the germination criteria so that testing can be performed on a regular basis.

When it comes to saving seeds, there are lots of steps and procedures to be followed to ensure you are successfully saving the best variety of seeds. This book, *Saving Seeds Handbook*, was written to be your compass and to provide you with virtually all you need to thrive as you journey into the practice of saving seeds in your garden. So, ensure you pay close attention to the points discussed in the pages of this book as we take a deep dive into the practice of saving seeds.

So, let's jump right into it!

# Chapter 1

# The Basics of Saving Seeds

**What is a Seed?**

You're probably familiar with seeds if you've ever eaten an apple or a watermelon. If those seeds are planted underground well enough, they will grow into plants like apple trees or watermelons.

The seed is the plant's embryonic stage. Embryo, the endosperm, and the seed coat make up most seeds. The embryo is a stem, root, and leaf plant. The endosperm is the seed's nutritional component, made up of oil, protein, and starch. The seed coat protects the seeds and keeps them viable for longer.

While humans usually avoid seeds in juicy fruits, many common dry foods contain seeds, such as lentils, peanuts, peas, and beans. Nuts like filberts, pecans, cashews, and walnuts are technically fruits, but we consume the seed and discard the fruit (or shell). Brazil nuts, almonds, and Pine nuts are all seeds, despite not being a nut. Spices like mustard, fenugreek, and nutmeg are seeds. Chocolate and coffee are two of our favorite non-legume "beans." How about cereal grains, corn, and rice? Grains contain seeds united to the ovary wall, therefore they are fruits, even though we eat them more for their nutritional worth. Not to worry: flax, puppy, and pumpkin seeds are all seeds as well.

**Types of Seeds**

Seeds are categorized into two categories based on;

1. The number of cotyledons present: The seeds with just one cotyledon on the exterior are known as monocotyledonous. Orchids, Alisma, maize, rice, and other crops are examples. The seeds with two cotyledons on both sides of the seed husk are known as dicotyledonous seeds. Examples include gram, pea, bean, mustard, mango, and so forth.

2. Whether or not a seed has endosperm, it may be divided into the following categories:

    Albuminous seeds (Endospermic): These are seeds that include endosperm, as the name suggests. Albuminous seeds have thin, membrane-like cotyledons, and the endosperm survives and feeds the seedling throughout its early stages of development. Plants like castor, poppy, custard apple, and others are examples.

Exalbuminous seeds (non-endospermic): Exalbuminous seeds or non-endospermic seeds do not have endosperm. At an early stage of development, food accumulates in the endosperm tissue of exalbuminous seeds but is devoured by the expanding embryo and mature seeds that do not possess endosperm. In these type of seeds, the cotyledons are food storage organs that develop fleshly and thick characteristics. Gram, pea, bean, and other legumes are examples.

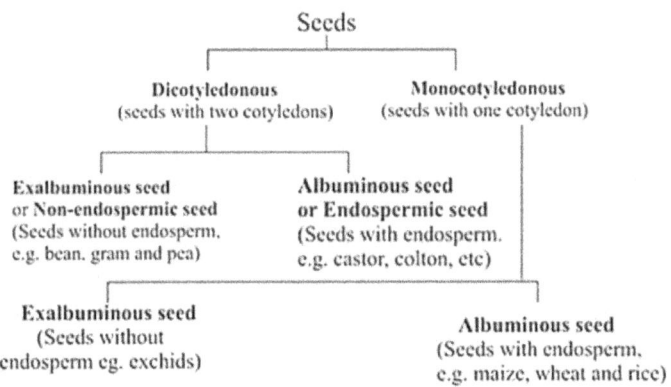

## Anatomy of Seed

The seed structures of monocotyledonous and dicotyledonous plants are distinct. Let's take a closer look at these structures:

### 1. Monocotyledonous Seed Structure

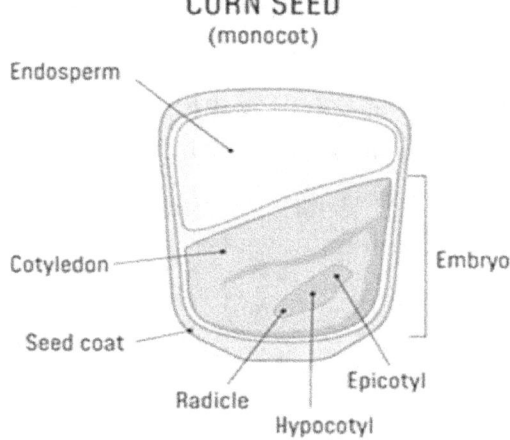

There is just one cotyledon in a monocotyledonous seed. The seed coat has just one outer coating. A good example is maize grain. It has a flat, almost triangular shape. Externally, it is divided into two areas: a big top region that identifies the endosperm's location and a little lower portion that houses the embryo. A substantial epithelial layer separates the two.

The following is its detailed structure:

Seed Coat: The seed coat of cereals such as maize is membranous and often united with the fruit wall (pericarp), known as Hull or Husk.

Endosperm: Food is stored in the endosperm. Monocot seeds are generally endospermic; however, few outliers exist, such as orchids, which are non-endospermic.

Aleurone layer: This proteinous layer separates the embryo from the endosperm's outer coat.

Embryo: The embryo is a little fleshy body found in a groove at one end of the endosperm after removing the seed coat. The embryo is made up of the following components:

   a. Cotyledon: Monocots only have one cotyledon. In monocots, such as grasses, the scutellum is the analogous structure.
   b. Plumule: The embryonic leaves and the developing tip of the shoot are represented by the plumule. It is encased in a sheath known as the coleoptile.
   c. Radicle: A radicle is a root cap-covered structure located at the base of a seed. The radicle's

undifferentiated protective coating is known as coleorhiza.

## 2. Dicotyledonous Seed Structure

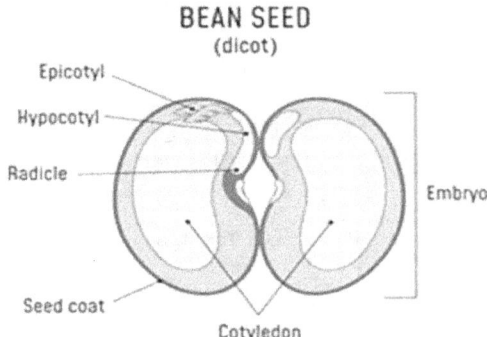

Two cotyledons are found in dicotyledonous seeds. Dicot seeds include peas, almonds, and cashews, to name a few. The following is the precise structure of a dicot seed (for example, a bean):

Seed Coat: Each seed has a seed coat that protects it from the elements. It develops from the ovule's integuments. An outer testa and an inner tegmen distinguish the seed coat.

   a. Testa is the thick, protective coating on the outside. It defends the seed against infections such as fungus, bacteria, and insects.

b. Tegman is a thin membrane inner coating covering the seed's inner component.
c. Hilum: The growing seed is linked to the fruit by a scar on the seed coat.
d. Micropyle: Above the hilum, there is a tiny pore called a micropyle. It's where water, oxygen, and other nutrients enter the seed.
e. Raphe: The median groove is surrounded by a ridge-like structure called Raphe. It denotes the part of the stalk that is still fused to the testa.

Embryo: It has two cotyledons and an embryonal axis.

a. Cotyledons: Dicots contain two cotyledons, which are food-filled and fleshy structures linked to the embryonal axis. In the early stages of development, they offer sustenance to the embryo.
b. Embryonal axis: The embryonal axis is a tiny plant that exists between the two distinct cotyledons. It comprises the following sections:

   I. Plumule: The plumule is the part of the plant that gives rise to the shoot.
   II. Radicle: The bottom section of the embryo that gives rise to roots is known as the radicle.

## How Are Seeds Formed?

Fertilization is a process that occurs in flowering plants. The ovule develops into a seed after fertilization, while the ovary matures into a fruit.

- The ovule becomes the seed
- The ovary becomes the fruit

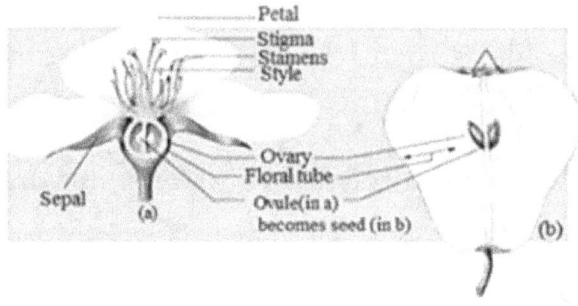

Fertilization is a sexual reproduction process in plants that occur after pollination and germination. Flowers, being the reproductive structures of angiosperms (flowering plants), play an important part in the fertilization process. Male gametes (the reproductive cell of an organism) are delivered into female reproductive organs by pollinators (butterflies, honey bees, bats, birds, flower beetles, etc.) during fertilization, and the end result is the creation of an embryo in a seed.

Below are the summarized processes that occur during seed formation:

1. The fertilized egg (zygote) divides numerous times within the ovule to become an embryo.
2. The ovule forms a strong sheath around it and is transformed over time into a seed that contains the infant plant.
3. The flower's ovary matures into a fruit with seeds inside.
4. The sepals, stamen, petals, stigma, and style of the flower all dry out and fall off.
5. Fruit can now be seen where there was a flower, and fruits contain the seed. Some plants, such as mangoes and oranges, produce delicious, soft, succulent fruits, while others, such as peanuts and almonds, produce dry, hard fruits.

## Saving Seeds Terminology

Annual: a plant that goes through its entire life cycle in one growing season, including germination, reproduction, and death. The pollen-producing portion of a stamen is called an anther.

Biennial: a plant that requires vernalization and typically completes its life cycle in two growing seasons, developing vegetatively in the first, vernalizing, producing flowers and seeds in the second, and dying in the third.

Bolt: to rapidly extend (as a stalk) before blossoming. Pollen from one plant is transferred to the stigma or flower of another plant, resulting in cross-pollination.

Cultivar: a plant or a collection of plants that have been bred or selected for distinct, desirable characteristics, also known as a variety.

F1: an abbreviation for "first filial generation"; the first-generation offspring produced from a cross between two separate populations or kinds.

Filament: The hairy stalk of a stamen with a pollen-bearing anther at its tip is called a filament.

Flower: Angiosperm's reproductive structure is called a flower.

GMO (genetically modified organism): an organism whose genetic makeup has been altered by molecular breeding techniques.

Germination. The process by which a seed collects water and swells, causing the radicle to break through the seed covering, resulting in an infant plant emerging from the seed.

Heirloom variety: an open-pollinated cultivar that has been passed down through a family or community from generation to generation.

Hybrid: hybrid is a plant or cultivar generated by crossing two stable, genetically different parental populations; it is also known as an F1 hybrid.

Isolation: the process of separating one plant or group of plants from another in order to avoid cross-pollination.

Natural selection is a multigenerational process in which heritable qualities become more or less frequent in a population due to how well those features enable individuals to survive and reproduce.

Open-pollinated variety: a variety that produces offspring with the variety's characteristic qualities when permitted to cross-pollinate exclusively with other members of the same population.

Perennial: a plant that can live for more than two years and produces flowers and seeds for a long time.

Pistil: the female reproductive organ in the center of a flower, consisting of an ovary, style, and stigma.

Pollen: anthers create pollen, which are dust-like particles that transport male reproductive cells in blooming plants.

Pollinator: a pollinator is an animal, usually an insect, that transports pollen from an anther to a stigma.

Population: a group of interfertile plants growing together with the ability to interbreed; the total number of plants of a variety that contribute their genetic material to the seeds being harvested;

Row cover: is a spun synthetic cloth that is used to protect crops against pests and cold.

Seed: a mature plant ovule with an embryo, endosperm, and seed coat is called a seed.

Seedborne: refers to infections or diseases that are carried in or on a seed.

Self-pollination: pollen transfer from an anther to a stigma of the same plant is known as self-pollination.

Stamen: a filament and an anther make up a stamen, which is the male reproductive component of a flower.

Stigma: The stigma is the sticky tip on the pistil that attracts pollen.

True-to-type: adhering to a given plant variety's known traits.

Variety: within a species, variety refers to a phenotypically diverse plant population occurring naturally: "Cultivar" is a term that is frequently used as a synonym.

Vernalization: is the process of exposing a plant to cold temperatures in order for it to blossom.

Last frost date: the day of the year (in most places, generally in late winter or early spring) when the air temperature is no longer projected to drop below the freezing point of water. Many seed-starting calculators assume that you will sow or plant a particular number of weeks following the last frost. Last frost-based planting calculations are only useful in mild-winter places like the Pacific Northwest.

First frost date: the day of the year (in most places, generally in the autumn) when the air temperature is projected to drop below the freezing point of water for the first time. The number of weeks before the first frost date is typically used in fall garden seed starting calculators to determine when to sow or plant. First frost-based planting estimates are only useful in mild-winter locations like the Pacific Northwest.

Days to maturity: days to harvest is another name for days to maturity, which is the number of days it takes a plant to reach harvestable size in theory. This figure varies greatly depending on the plant's growth environment. The number of days it takes a plant to develop and mature is affected by several factors, including the time of year, heat units, day length, sun intensity, soil fertility, soil texture, moisture stress, insect and disease stress, weed competition, crowding, seed age at sowing, and a million more. For plants that are not normally direct-seeded, such as tomatoes or eggplant, many seed catalogs specify days to maturity from the time of transplant.

The nearer a seed house is to your garden, the more precise the days to maturity estimate will be; however, it's preferable to use this number to compare various varieties of a crop.

Direct sowing: planting seeds directly in the soil where the plant will develop is known as direct sowing. Direct seeding is nearly required for plants cultivated for their roots, such as beets, carrots, and parsnips, and is favored for many crops that are simple to sow, such as peas and beans, but difficult to transfer, such as squash.

Seed starting: refers to the practice of planting seeds at a site different from the plant's final growth location with the aim of transplanting the resulting seedling at a later date. Seeds may be started outdoors, in a greenhouse, beneath seed lights, or close to a window. Flats, pots, and other containers are often used to start them.

Specialty seed starting mix is often utilized. Seeds are started for several purposes, including vegetables that require a growing season longer than the average, ensuring regular spacing in the garden, encouraging greater seed germination rates, and more.

Hardening off: is the process of progressively acclimating a seedling from a sheltered habitat to the conditions of the outside environment before it is transplanted. For example, before transplanting a seedling outdoors, that was grown in a greenhouse, expose it to increased hours of colder wind and temperatures.

Transplanting: is the process of moving a plant from one place to another. This typically refers to taking a seedling out of its pot and planting it in its final location in the vegetable garden. If you can dig it up and put it someplace else, any plant, including trees and shrubs, has the possibility of transplanting.

**Why Save Seeds?**

Many people are attempting gardening for the first time this year or extending gardens they already have. We're trying to get some more people to start saving seed as well! Here are ten reasons why you should try to save some seed this year, whether you're a backyard gardener or a farmer.

1. Maintaining diversity in genetics

Farmers and gardeners have lost much control over seed storage and variety preservation in recent years. Seeds have become the exclusive domain of a few large corporations. These businesses concentrate on only a few kinds of each crop. We are losing more and more types as farmers and gardeners cease conserving seed.

**What is the significance of this?**

While we adore all of our open-pollinated and heirloom varieties for many reasons, including flavor, beauty, and frost resistance, to mention but a few, we also recognize that we may require a variety's specific attributes at some point in the future. Take, for example, Gourdseed Corn. It was on the verge of extinction by the 1960s, as interest in hybrid corn surged. On the other hand, recently identified surviving cultivars have shown significant disease resistance, particularly to southern leaf blight.

2. Spending less

Seeds aren't the most costly item in the world, but if you have a large garden, they may quickly add up. Saving at least a few of your favorite types each year will help you save money. You might also come across a seed swap where you can trade for a few different types.

3. Connecting with your forefathers

You might be able to conserve seed from what your forefathers have been cultivating for years if you have older gardeners in the family. Thanks to the internet, you can also find heirlooms developed in locations where your ancestors originated, regardless of where you presently reside.

Growing some of your own food provides a living link to history, even if you have no idea who your ancestors were or what they grew. You can even create a new tradition by passing down seeds from an open-pollinated variety to your children.

4. Increase your self-sufficiency

Many people want to be self-sufficient during difficult times. Seed saving is a fantastic skill to learn!

5. Adapting seeds to your garden

You're steadily improving your garden if you save seeds from your best plants each year. Seeds in the future will be better adapted to grow in your specific climatic and soil circumstances.

6. Helping pollinators

More plants in your garden will be permitted to flower if you save seeds. Many pollinator-friendly plants, such as lettuce, radish, and basil, are easy to save seeds from.

7. Taking back control of open-pollinated seeds

When you preserve and exchange seeds, you assist in protecting everyone's right to conserve, grow, and breed plants.

8. Creating new varieties

You can try your hand at generating your own variety once you've mastered seed saving.

9. Controlling your supply of food

You know exactly what goes into your seeds and plants by saving seeds and starting your own plants, which is especially great for organic gardeners and farmers.

# Chapter 2

# Planning For Seed Production

**Choosing Seeds for Saving**

When selecting plants to save seeds from, seek those with the most vigor and health – those that yield fruits or veggies you enjoy eating or flowers you can't get enough of.

Keep in mind that not all plants generate seeds that are viable. Hybrids, which make up the majority of plants sold in garden centers, are made by artificially cross-pollinating cultivars and will not yield plants that are true to type. Hybrid seeds should not be saved. They will generate seedlings that look nothing like the parent plant and are almost never good. Avoid seed packs that contain the phrases hybrid or F1, and if you wish to gather your plants' seeds, inquire before you buy.

If you want to achieve consistent results from seeds, search for open-pollinated plants. They are non-hybrid varieties that reproduce through either self or cross-pollination. If you save the seed from an open-pollinated plant and don't cross-pollinate it with another plant of the same species, it will breed true-to-type. All heritage seeds are pollinated by the wind.

Beans, peas, tomatoes, and lettuce are self-pollinating plants with flowers containing male and female parts. As a result, each flower can be nourished either by itself or another flower on the same plant nearby. Seed from self-pollinating plants almost always generates an identical plant. However, this does not account for the potential of pollen being transferred from one cultivar to the next by an insect.

**Note:** If pollen is carried from the flower of a self-pollinating plant to another, the seed generated by that flower will be distinct from the seed produced by all other flowers on the plant.

Cross-pollinated plants account for the bulk of vegetables grown in home gardens. Pollen from other plants in the same family can fertilize these cultivars, including squash, broccoli, and pepper. Cross-pollination between similar types growing nearby should be avoided while saving seed. Planting two types of radish in the garden, for example, will result in cross-pollination. The seed from these plants may or may not be what you're looking for, as each plant has distinct characteristics.

**Plant Life-Cycles**

It's relatively simple to save seeds from vegetables, flowers, and herbs. The plant's life cycle (annual, biennial, or perennial) will dictate when — and occasionally how — the seeds can be kept. Beans, tomatoes, basils, oregano, and marigold are all annuals that blossom and produce seeds in the same growing season. As a result, they are great plants for seed collection.

Because biennial plants do not generate seeds their first year, keep them protected over the winter and harvest their seeds at the conclusion of the next growing season. It will take a little longer to save biennial seeds from caraway, beets, evening primrose, Swiss chard, and onion, but if they do not cross-pollinate with similar cultivars, their seed will yield plants that are true to type.

Plants like daisies, rhubarb, artichokes, chives, and mint are perennials that come back year after year. Perennial plants, while frequently propagated from seed, are reproduced often from cuttings or division.

## Planning Your Population Size

If you're growing a plant variety for seed, you should consider how many plants you'll need to produce a good yield. This entails more than simply gathering enough seeds; it also entails effectively conserving the DNA of the variety by saving seeds from multiple plants. We typically assume that plants are similar because they look similar, but they might be quite distinct in ways we don't perceive. Consider a row of lettuce, for example. If all the lettuce plants have the same shape and color leaves, and the heads are all approximately the same size and shape, and they all taste the same, you'd think they're all genetically identical. You'd assume that by taking seeds from a single plant, you'd be able to preserve all of the features of that kind.

**Unfortunately, the answer is no.**

Those plants are all the same variety because they were all chosen for their shape, color, and flavor. In other words, a seed grower combed through their lettuce row in the past and plucked all the plants with diverse forms, colors, and tastes, leaving only the plants that are uniform-looking to go to seed. That's why they all now have the same appearance and flavor. However, they did not exclude any plants based on other traits such as drought tolerance, disease resistance, seed lifetime, root vitality, and so on. This implies that some of the "uniform" plants are drought tolerant, have better root systems, and produce longer-lasting seeds than others.

You can observe these characteristics sometimes, but not always. You can notice which plants develop better during a drought, for example. However, if it has recently rained, the drought-tolerant plants appear identical to the others. Disease resistance is fantastic, but you can't determine which plants are disease-resistant unless the others are sick. You can evaluate the plant from above, but you won't know which plants have the most extensive root systems unless you dig down with a very little spade and inspect them for yourself. These "invisible" characteristics are crucial, but they go unnoticed most of the time.

Suddenly, your lettuce row does not appear to be as uniform as it once was. How can you know if you're collecting strong root genetics, good seed storage genetics, and good disease resistance genetics if you only take seeds from one plant? Maybe you'll pick a plant that doesn't have any of these qualities, and your lettuce will be weaker and of worse quality for the most part afterward. When you store seeds from a large number of plants at once, you're ensuring that the best genes survive, even if you can't see their benefits. Sure, you'll also gather the lesser hidden genes, but at least you'll avoid losing the powerful ones. Stronger genes will survive and dominate in the future; thus, they're worth maintaining at any cost.

So, how many plants are needed to save seeds so as to acquire a variety's entire secret genetics? Consider the following scenario: you have a bag of colored marbles and wish to take a handful from it with at least one of each color. How big of a handful will ensure that you obtain at least one marble of each color? The answer is contingent on the number of colors present. The same approach is utilized to establish a minimum population size in population genetics, along with some complex math. That is the minimal number of plants from which you should harvest seeds in order to be certain of collecting all of a variety's DNA.

Recommended minimum population sizes for commercial seed production:

- 40 plants of bush beans
- 20 cucumber plants
- 20 lettuce plants
- 20 pepper plants (sweet)
- 20 tomato plants

This is the minimal number of plants from which a commercial seed planter should save seeds in order to be 95 percent certain of retaining each variety's complete DNA. Commercial growers frequently produce more, although these figures may appear to be excessive for a home seed saver.

For the home garden scale, the community norms for personal seed-saving appear to be more reasonable:

- 20 plants of bush beans
- 6 cucumber plants
- 6 plants of lettuce
- 6 pepper plants (sweet)

- 6 tomato plants

The distinction is that while the community standard will almost always provide good outcomes, there is no assurance that unique qualities will be inherited from one generation to the next, and the variety may weaken with time.

## Isolation of Varieties

In seed saving, maintaining a variety's distinctive features is critical, and isolation is one of three fundamental facets (together with population size control and selection) required to successfully conserve true-to-type seeds. Isolation is the most important method for keeping variations true to type since it eliminates undesirable cross-pollination. Isolation begins with an awareness of the distance required to reduce or eliminate the possibility of cross-pollination between two species variations.

Isolation can be achieved in a variety of ways, including distance, barrier, timing, and bagging. The most widely used method is isolation by distance, which includes putting enough space between a variety and any pollen sources to guarantee that the variety remains true to type. The next section delves into the various isolation techniques.

## Methods of Isolation

Although various animal species seldom hybridize or only with considerable difficulty and (quite plainly) by chance, plants, on the other hand, are the total opposite. While certain plants will not cross with others, many of them will. Even if you're cultivating plants that don't cross-pollinate, there's a good possibility you're growing multiple varieties of a plant that does. If you're preserving your own seed and don't want to rely on the luck of what will come forth next year, you'll want to take some precautions to avoid natural cross-pollination.

While being a home gardener doesn't give the luxury of hundreds of feet (or, in some cases, kilometers) between our types, or plants, there are precautions that even the tiniest-space home gardener may take to avoid cross-pollination. It's vital to remember that nearby neighbors may produce crops that cross-pollinate with yours. Let's take a look at the different methods of isolation.

**By Distance**

The distance separating your different plants, or different species of a similar plant, is simply the distance separating them to prevent cross-pollination by animals, wind, or insects. The USDA (US Department of Agriculture) has provided the following recommendations to guarantee the purity of seed between different plants and types of variety.

| | |
|---|---|
| Bean (Common, Fava, Lima) | 40 metres (1320 ft) |
| Beet | 8 kilometres (5 miles) |
| Brussels Sprouts | 200 metres (660 ft) |
| Cabbage | 200 metres (660 ft) |
| Cantaloupe | 40 metres (1320 ft) |
| Carrot | 40 metres (1320 ft) |
| Cauliflower | 200 metres (660 ft) |
| Corn | 40 metres (1320 ft) |
| Cucumber | 40 metres (1320 ft) |
| Eggplant | N/A* |
| Lettuce | N/A* |
| Pea | N/A* |
| Pepper (Hot, Sweet) | 9 metres (30 ft) |
| Potato | 9 metres (30 ft) |
| Squash (Summer, Winter, Pumpkin) | 40 metres (1320 ft) |
| Radish | 40 metres (1320 ft) |
| Spinach | 8 kilometres (5 miles) |
| Tomatillo | 9 metres (30 ft) |
| Tomato | 9 metres (30 ft) |
| Turnip | 200 metres (660 ft) |
| Watermelon | 40 metres (1320 ft) |

*Note that while the USDA does not consider distance to be necessary, these figures are based on crops produced in vast quantities in fields instead of inter-plantings common in home gardens. Personally, I will recommend the barrier approach of isolation, especially if several types are produced in close proximity.

It's worth remembering that planting groups of different plants/varieties close together increases the likelihood of cross-pollination. Consider this and use a time isolation method or a barrier method to ensure that your seed comes out as "true" because this is how the majority of home gardeners grow their crops.

## By Barrier

The barrier approach involves creating a physical barrier that separates your plants or varieties to prevent pollen from being transferred from one to the other by pollinators or wind. It's worth noting that while putting a barrier between two distinct species or crops, such as a wall or your house, can reduce cross-pollination, it's far from guaranteed, especially if the distances separating plants are near.

## Bagging

Bagging is a very easy and effective strategy to prevent cross-pollination. I like purchasing meters of pre-made, low-cost organza bags from craft stores and use them as is. Before the flowers blossom, use these bags to wrap around the buds (this is critical!).

Leave the bag in place until the plants begin to bear fruit. You can't guarantee 100 percent seed purity if the bag is tied on after the flowers have opened or removed before the blossoms have completely died off. Because no hand-pollination is required, this strategy is best for plants that are either self-pollinating or self-fertilizing. Self-fertilizing plants include tomatoes, beans, and peppers. You can also use paper bags for this, but because they aren't see-through, you'll have to undo and retie the flower cluster's bag on a regular basis. Don't use plastic since it can produce a climate that is too hot for the fruit to set correctly.

A note about squash: the bagging procedure is suggested to keep squash types pure because they cross quickly (and, in fact, pollen from the male flower must be deposited inside the female bloom).

**Caging**

Caging is similar to bagging, but rather than isolate separate clusters of flowers, a box is constructed that may be placed over the entire plant and secured with a metal skeleton or wood and mesh (tulle and fine screen door netting are great choices for this).

**By Time**

Time isolation necessitates meticulous planning. It requires employing varying maturity rates or staggered planting to time your plants to bloom at different times. As an outcome, pollinators trade pollen that is either unsuited or entirely pollen from that plant's blossoms when they arrive. This is a great option for plants that need pollination from flowers other than their own, such as tomatillos, but it doesn't account for neighbors that plant various plants or varieties that are compatible with yours.

**Hand Pollination**

Pollination is still required to establish seeds in crops that are already isolated to prevent cross-pollination. As a result, you can pollinate plants by hand instead of relying on insect pollinators. Hand pollination is simple to do with crops like corn and squash, but it is not commonly done on larger-scale gardens or farms due to the time commitment involved.

If you want to hand pollinate, you should do so if:

- Bees and other insects aren't swarming around your floral plants.

- You are growing in a greenhouse, indoors, or on a screened-in porch.
- Your plants produce fruit that shrivels and perishes before having a chance to mature.

Even if pollinators are active, you may want to consider manually pollinating to avoid cross-pollination between similar plants. This is crucial if you wish to keep seeds from your garden to grow more of the same plant, which is typical with heirloom types. In this post about seeds, learn more about the differences between heirlooms and hybrids.

## Hand Pollination Best Practices

There are two types of plants when it comes to hand pollination: those flowers are self-fertile and those with distinct male and female flowers.

- Pollination of Self-Fertile Plants

Plants that are self-fertile (also known as "self-pollinating" or "self-fruitful") include:

- ✓ Tomatoes
- ✓ Eggplants
- ✓ Beans

- ✓ Peppers
- ✓ Peas
- ✓ Strawberries

Use a little paintbrush to encourage pollen release in self-fertile plants like tomatoes. These plant's flowers have all of the components needed to bear fruit. If you're growing outdoors, hand pollination isn't normally essential because even a tiny breeze can help with pollination.

But, just in case, here are two methods for pollinating a self-fertile plant:

- ✓ To encourage pollen release, gently shake the plant or blow on its blossoms (flowers)
- ✓ Alternatively, to transport pollen into the pistil, gently swab the inside of each bloom (flower) with a little paintbrush or cotton swab (center section of the flower).

- ■ Pollinating Plants With The Male and Female Flowers Separated

Plants that produce male and female flowers separately on the same plant include the following.

- ✓ Cucumbers
- ✓ Pumpkins
- ✓ Cantaloupes
- ✓ Watermelons
- ✓ Squash
- ✓ Zucchini

Pollen from a male bloom must reach a female flower in order for these plants to bear fruit. As a result, these crops have a harder time pollinating than self-fertile plants.

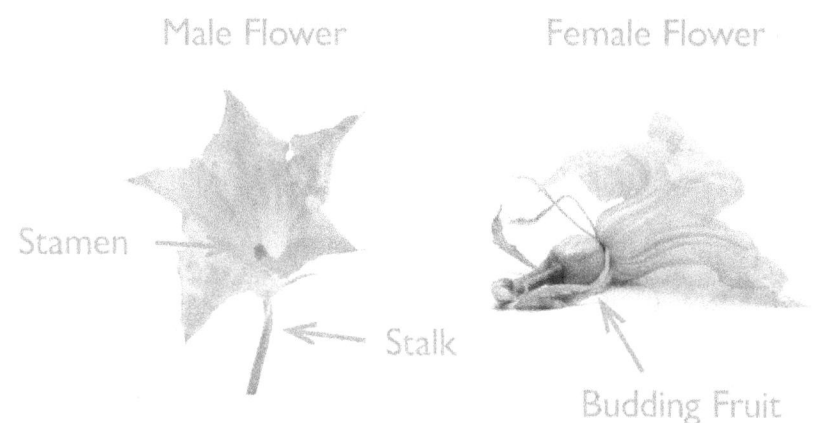

Male flowers (with short stalks and stamens that are laden with pollen) bloom early in most cases. These bloom for a few days and then fall off. Female blooms should begin to appear after a few weeks (which typically comes with little budding fruits at the base).

*Squash, cucumbers, and other cucurbit plants produce male and female flowers individually.*

Pollination is easier in the morning while the blooms are open. Use the following techniques to do so:

- ✓ Using a small paintbrush or cotton swab, swab the inside of the male flower, then swab the inside of the female flower to transfer pollen; or
- ✓ Pick a male bloom, peel off its petals, then use the male stamen to lightly sprinkle pollen onto the pistils of the females.

## Growing Seeds – Indoor or Outdoor

### Indoor Seed Planting

The Good: You have the most control over your seedlings when you start them indoors. You can quickly monitor your seeds' germination rate and provide additional moisture or warmth as needed. Seedlings are less susceptible to pests and diseases in a controlled environment.

The Bad: Indoor seed starting necessitates a sufficient amount of space in a somewhat warm room, as well as, at the absolute least, a bright window, preferably facing south. If you just have a cold, dark basement and don't want to invest in an indoor grow light system, you're better off buying seedling plugs or starter plants or waiting until you can sow your seeds outside.

## How to Start Planting Seeds Indoor

Ensure your seed planting pots have enough light by placing them in front of a sunny window that gets at least eight hours of light per day.

## Needed Supplies

- ✓ Seeds
- ✓ Starter mix for seeds
- ✓ Mixing container; large
- ✓ Seeding using small containers or pots
- ✓ Drainage can be achieved using a plastic plant tray, a baking sheet, or any other suitable "saucer."
- ✓ Plant markers
- ✓ Spray bottle with a fine mist

## Instructions

- ✓ Fill the big container halfway with water and add your seed-starter mix. Before you begin, you want to make sure that all of the water has been absorbed and that the mix is moist.

- ✓ After spreading the seed starting mixture into each small container, place them in your plant tray, and leave about ½ inch at the top.
- ✓ Spread some seeds (3 to 4 if they're large, or a fair amount if they are small) over the seed starting mixture. Carry on with the rest of the containers and seeds in the same manner. Make sure each container is properly labeled.
- ✓ Cover the seeds with seed starting mix according to the seed packet's directions. In general, coat the seeds with a thin layer commensurate to their height, ranging from 1/8" to ½" or higher. Because certain seeds want light to sprout, they don't need to be covered at all. Just press them into the seed starting mixture.
- ✓ Gently push down the seed starting mixture with your fingertips (or using a spoon's back), then sprinkle the surface thoroughly with your spray bottle.

✓ Set the plant tray, as well as all the containers your just seeded, in a sunny spot in a warm location. Keep the seed starting mixture evenly moist until the seedlings are appropriate to be transferred into your garden. To avoid harming your seedlings or displacing the seeds while growing, it's advisable to use the spray bottle.

### Getting Your Seedlings to Harden Off

Your seedlings will need to undergo a basic "hardening off" process before being transplanted outside. Hardening off means to acclimate your plants to the outdoors to withstand the sun, wind, cold, and other elements they weren't exposed to while growing indoors.

Once your seedlings have grown two to three sets of leaves, you can begin hardening them off. They're old enough to go outside at that point.

- ✓ Take your seedlings outside around 7 to 10 days before they are set to be transplanted, placing them under a shade for some time, either in the morning or afternoon. Afterward, take them in before the sun sets—repeat for an extra day or two. If the weather is particularly cold or windy, suspend the seedling-hardening off process until the weather improves.

- ✓ For some hours, either in the morning or afternoon, position the seedlings in shaded sunlight following their two-to-three-day debut to the outer world. Take them in before the sun sets – repeat for an additional day or two. After that, place them outside in direct sunlight for the entire day, bringing them inside before dusk. Repeat the process the next day.

- ✓ If the weather is really hot, give your seedlings some shade or shift them into partial shade during the hottest portion of the day.
- ✓ Finally, until your seedlings are set to be transferred into the garden, allow them to spend the entire day and night outside.

**Outdoor Seed Planting**

The Good: If your soil has been prepared, outdoor seed planting is quick and easy. It's a natural method to garden, and it lets the seeds decide when to sprout, whether you're sowing all your crops in tidy and evenly spaced rows or disseminating handfuls of flower seeds over a large area.

The Bad: If you're not careful with watering, the weather not cooperating, or a critter digging up your newly seeded beds, outdoor seed planting can be difficult and unpredictable. During the first few weeks, watch out for weeds that could compete with the seedlings.

## How to Start Planting Seeds Outdoor

Whether you're growing in the ground, raised beds, or containers, start with properly prepared soil.

## Needed Supplies

- ✓ Seeds
- ✓ Furrows, which can be made with a trowel, hand hoe, or weeder
- ✓ Plant markers
- ✓ A hose that has a spray nozzle, sprinkler, or watering can

**Instructions**

- ✓ Wet the soil thoroughly until it is drained and saturated in the first few inches.

- ✓ Instructions on how deep to sow your seeds and how far apart to space them can be found on the seed packets. Make a shallow furrow in the dirt with your desired tool.

- ✓ In the furrow, place the seeds at the recommended spacing.

- ✓ Return the soil to the furrow, sweeping it over the seeds and gently tamping it down with your tool. Each seeded row should be labeled.

- ✓ Water the soil lightly with a moderate spray, taking care not to suffocate the seeds. Depending on the weather, you might have to water once daily or twice daily to ensure the soil is moist until the germination of your seeds. Reduce the amount of watering as the seedlings grow and their roots become more entrenched.

## Seeds to Plant Indoor or Outdoor

Starting plants from seed is a fun and cost-effective way to produce veggies, herbs, and fruit for your yard. When planting, many new gardeners start with transplants from a local nursery or garden center. While there is nothing wrong with purchasing plants, it can be costly and offer limited options. Even the most seasoned gardener is astounded by the variety of seed options available. Tomatoes, for example, come in hundreds of varieties, all of which may be produced from seed.

Starting seeds indoors doesn't require a greenhouse, but it does require potting soil, pots or flats, and space to grow until the seedlings are ready to be transplanted into the garden. Is it necessary to sow all seeds indoors, or can some be put straight in the garden? Because I enjoy planting directly into the garden, I've researched which vegetable and herb seeds can be directly grown into the soil over the years. The table below will assist you in determining which seeds must be grown indoors and which can be planted outside when the time comes.

## Seeds to sow in the garden (outdoor)

| Chicory | Lovage | Spinach |
|---|---|---|
| Chinese Cabbage | Mache-Corn Salad | Sorrel |
| Calendula | Marjoram | Summer and Winter Squash |
| Caraway | Mesclun Salad Mix | Sunflower |
| Carrots | Millet | Swiss Chard |
| Turnips | Watermelon | |

| Anise | Cilantro | Mustard Greens |
| --- | --- | --- |
| Arugula | Collards Greens | Nasturtium |
| Pole Beans | Comfrey | Okra |
| Bush Beans | Sweet Corn | Bunching Onions |
| Fava Beans | Cucumber | Onions-Cippolina |
| Beets | Dill | Parsley |
| Bok Choy | Endive | Parsnips |
| Broccoli | Fennel | Peas |
| Brussels Sprouts | Kale | Pumpkin |
| Brussels Sprouts | Kohlrabi | Radish |
| Cabbage | Leek | Rutabaga |
| Chervil | Lettuce | Salsify |
| Chicory | Lovage | Spinach |

## Seed to sow indoor

- ✓ Celery
- ✓ Celeriac
- ✓ Mint
- ✓ Oregano
- ✓ Onion (some varieties)
- ✓ Peppers
- ✓ Rosemary

- ✓ Strawberry
- ✓ Thyme
- ✓ Tomatoes
- ✓ Sage
- ✓ Eggplant
- ✓ Lavender
- ✓ Lemon Balm
- ✓ Tomatillos

## Seed to sow, whether indoor or outdoor

- ✓ Amaranth
- ✓ Artichoke
- ✓ Basil
- ✓ Cabbage
- ✓ Cauliflower
- ✓ Chives
- ✓ Amaranth
- ✓ Amaranth
- ✓ Artichoke
- ✓ Basil
- ✓ Artichoke
- ✓ Basil
- ✓ Cress (watercress)
- ✓ Leek

- ✓ Melon
- ✓ Peanuts

For different reasons, some plants are simply too difficult to grow from seed. Flavored mints, such as chocolate mint, do not grow "true to seed," meaning that the plant's seed will not return to a regular mint. It can be grown by planting divisions from the parent plant or rooting parts of the plant in soil.

Another plant that cannot be produced from seed is French tarragon. The sterile flowers are small. This variety of tarragon must be grown from plant cuttings or divisions. Sometimes a Russian tarragon or a Mexican tarragon is used instead, but the flavor isn't the same. There are other veggies that are cultivated from the vegetable's own parts, such as the roots or crowns. Some plants, such as lemongrass and rhubarb, can be grown from seed, but it is notoriously difficult. Asparagus can be grown from seed, but it will take years before it is ready to harvest. One-year-old crowns will give it a head start, therefore over planting seed is often recommended.

Asparagus, garlic, and other herbs and vegetables like the ones below are among them.

- ✓ Horseradish
- ✓ Rhubarb
- ✓ Lemon
- ✓ Verbena
- ✓ Artichoke of Jerusalem
- ✓ Lemongrass
- ✓ Potato
- ✓ Sweet Potato

Going over the above lists should give you a decent sense of what veggies and herbs you can grow from seed, whether it is indoors or outdoors. If you want to cultivate any of the plants that are grown in other ways, you'll be able to incorporate them into your garden design.

In order to grow a thriving garden, you must first plan. Begin by making a plant wish list, then determining whether it's feasible based on your budget, time and space constraints, climate, soil, and location. You'll discover that organization and planning are key to a successful and enjoyable garden season.

# Chapter 3

# Harvesting Mature Seeds

You should carefully harvest seeds if you want high-quality seeds. The seeds should have the characteristics of the planted variety. If a long purple eggplant, for example, is grown, the harvested fruit should have these characteristics.

## Harvesting Guidelines

Below are the guidelines you should follow when harvesting mature seeds;

- ✓ Only save seeds from the highest-quality plants you've identified for preservation. Flowers or leaves from these plants should not be picked. You're merely raising them for the seed.
- ✓ Organza, paper bags, or old stockings can be used to cover seed heads. Tie a string around the stalk to keep the seeds safe from the wind and predators.
- ✓ As you collect and replace pots, use plant labels to identify each seed variety. Many seeds

resemble each other, making it simple to misplace or confuse them.
- ✓ Before collecting seeds, they must be fully mature. When the seed heads or the entire plant are nearly ripe, take them off and dry them undercover or let them dry completely on the plant before harvesting.
- ✓ If you plant seeds that have been harvested before their prime, they will typically sprout if planted right away. Those seeds that have the most time to store more nutrients, on the other hand, survive the longest when stored.
- ✓ When the dew has evaporated, harvest seeds or fruit containing seeds about 10 a.m., when they are dry.
- ✓ To avoid mold or premature germination, seed heads requiring drying prior to seed extraction should be fully dried after collection.

## Supply List for Harvesting Seeds

- ✓ For seed collection, use sharp secateurs.
- ✓ For collecting and winnowing, use buckets, containers, and trays
- ✓ Use tarps or geotextile drop cloths to dry seed heads, capture seed, or winnow onto

- ✓ To extract the chaff and filter water from wet seeds, use fine mesh strainers of various sizes or use sieves instead.
- ✓ Clean seeds using a pastry brush, cloth bags, and rolling pin
- ✓ If there isn't enough wind to winnow, use a box fan.
- ✓ Ferment and process wet seeds using jars or tiny containers.
- ✓ To dry seeds, employ the use of string and paper bags, plates, trays, or glass.
- ✓ Use pen markers and labels to keep track of seed varieties when you collect and process seeds.

**Timing The Harvest**

Seed harvesting is a delicate balancing act. You want the seeds to be fully matured, so you want them to be as ripe as possible. Because of wet weather, seed loss, or hungry animals, if mature seed pods disintegrate or air-borne seed heads are ripped up by the wind, you may choose to harvest sooner. It's not uncommon to harvest some dry seed heads before all of their seed has dried and matured. Before they can be processed, they will need further time to 'cure.'

After seeds start drying on the plant, overhead watering or rain may further degrade seed quality. You may have to wait until the seed heads have completely dried following the rain. However, there's a chance they'll be overripe by then. The seed must be dry and firm enough to withstand being processed, and the material of the plant to which it is attached must be delicate enough to fracture and detach from the seed easily. To get your timing as close to perfect as possible, you'll need to pay attention to what stage your plants are in. If several seed harvests aren't possible, find a middle ground between having to wait for later developing seed to ripen and selecting early maturing seed lest several of them comes off the plant or gets too fragile, breaking during harvest. As a general rule, collect when 60-80 percent of your seeds are mature.

Each herb and vegetable has its own method for detecting when the seeds or fruit are ready to be harvested. There are two types of crops: dry seeded and wet seeded. It takes a little skill and experience to recognize the characteristics of each plant so you can harvest at the correct time, but there are some general rules.

Now, let's talk about dry and wet seeded crops regarding the time to harvest their seeds.

## Dry Seeded Crops

In these crops, seeds are found in husks, dried pods, or the seed-bearing portion of the plant. Some seeds can be plucked before being totally brown and dry if they are likely to be damaged by weather conditions, insects, rodents, or birds. The mustard family plants (Brassicaceae or Cruciferae), on the other hand, do not continue to ripen after harvesting. So, if at all feasible, let these seeds stay put on the plant until they are totally grown and dry (e.g., cabbage, broccoli, and kale).

Lastly, plants with shattering seed pods, such as lettuce and the carrot and onion families, must be plucked in stages as they ripen, especially if the weather is windy or damp since this can destroy or disperse the seeds (e.g., dill, spring onions, parsley, and chives). All 'dry seeded' crops have their seeds extracted using dry processing processes. When it comes to dry seeded crops, how can you determine when they are set to be harvested?

The following are some examples of indicators:

- ✓ The color of the seed pods/capsules, or the seeds themselves: The color of seeds can change as they mature and ripen, from white or green to yellow, light brown, or dark brown or black.

- ✓ The dryness of the pod or seed: Open the seed pod to determine the availability of some 'give' in it or if it is crispy and dried. If you extend the waiting period longer, the pods will fracture, and the seeds will fall out before you can harvest them.

- ✓ The ease with which the seed or seed pod can be isolated from the stalk: When the seed is ready, aggressively rub the head of the seed with crops such as beets, Swiss chard, or coriander to release the seed, which will easily come off when it's ripe.

Because seeds inside pods ripe and mature at various rates, each plant may have to be harvested individually when the time is right. It's ideal to check on your plants every day as they get closer to harvesting. Plants like lettuce and dill have seeds that ripen at different periods on the same plant. Without the loss of seeds, you can pluck out the entire plant and hang bags tied around the heads of the seed heads upturned to dry and ripen.

## Wet Seeded Crops

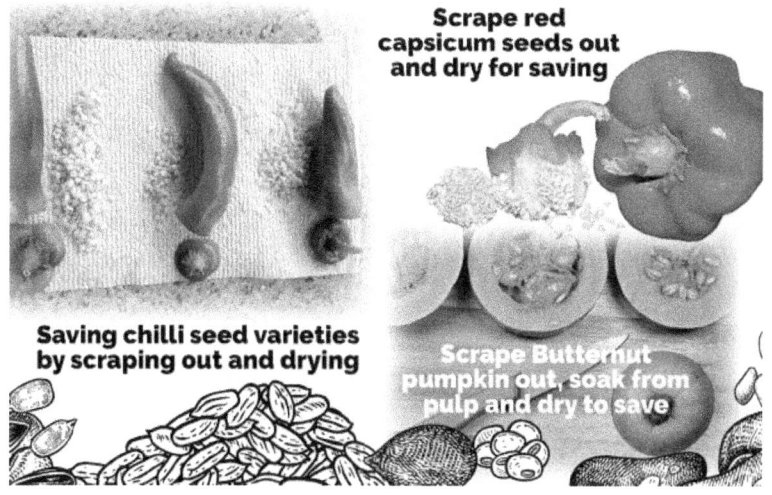

These seeds, which ripen within fruits that are fleshy come from the Solanaceae plant family (which includes eggplants, tomatoes, chilies, and capsicums) and the Cucurbitaceae plant family (which includes cucumbers, melons and squashes). Various wet seed processing procedures can be applied to pull off and dry these seeds. Again, there are hints to help you determine when to pluck your fruit in extracting the seeds that have matured. Let's take a look at some wet seeded crop's characteristics.

- ✓ Tomatoes and eggplant, which contain seeds in their pulp, are best to harvest when they are overripe, becoming soft, and just past being edible.

- ✓ Zucchini, cucumber, sweetcorn, and okra are frequently taken young for consumption, but they must achieve full maturity and then be set aside on the vine for about 3 weeks before the seeds mature.

- ✓ When capsicum and pumpkin have developed fully and are ready to eat, they are harvested. After picking, these crop seeds are scraped away from the cavity.

- ✓ For squash and pumpkin varieties, the seeds will keep growing in quality and size for many days, weeks, or even months after the fruit initially becomes edible. The germination rate increases as the seed mature. Picking the fruit to safeguard it from damage or disease and leaving it in storage to ripe before processing the seeds is sometimes necessary.

## Processing The Seeds

As a working space, a table in a dry, shielded undercover environment away from high humidity and wind is excellent.

Store immature seeds in bags, away from rats, to allow them to mature and ripe before being processed. Small amounts of seeds can be put on a plate and dried in a cool, shady, and well-ventilated location. Seed heads that are mature and have dry seeds can be processed right away. Fruit that contains seeds must be prepared separately.

The fruits and seeds, whether 'dry' or 'wet' when mature, will surely affect the seed cleaning process to be adopted.

## Processing Dry Seeds

*Winnowing by blowing chaff away from the seeds and out into the garden where stray seeds may self sow*

*Winnowing rice in the field using the wind to remove chaff*

When the seed heads of your plant have dried sufficiently, separate the seeds from the non-seed debris. Pods or husks (also called 'chaff'), stones, stems, insects, soil, leaves, and weed seeds are all examples of this. Tiny insects frequently eat seeds as they dry. The goal is to produce 'clean seed,' free of chaff and ready to be packaged and stored for a long time. Some seeds are simple to clean, while others require a little more effort.

Depending on the type of seed, cleaning can be done using one or more techniques:

- ✓ On the basis of weight, 'winnowing' separates seeds from plant material. Blowing air disperses the heavy seeds as they fall off the lighter chaff. One option is to scatter little amounts of seed material on a shallow tray and blow away the chaff with your breath. To capture any seeds blasted out, do this on a tablecloth or newspaper, and then hand-clean. To winnow larger amounts, drop the mixture of seed and chaff from a few feet atop a bucket or onto a tarp in front of a low-speed fan or cold hair drier. As the chaff is blown off, the seeds should fall into the pail. The same effect can be achieved by blowing a mild breeze.

- ✓ 'Screening' seeds with different-sized sieves, strainers, or screens over a tray or plate help separate them by size. Seeds fall into the tray, while chaff collects above on the screen or sieve. Use two screens, one that has the size of a mesh slightly smaller than the seeds and another whose mesh size is considerably bigger than the seeds.

Ensure any plant material that is smaller than the seeds falls off the initial screen by shaking and rubbing the seed against it. The seeds pass past the second screen, but anything larger is blocked. If you don't want any chaff, but a pure clean seed, you may need to repeat the process. Use a pastry brush to swiftly clean trays of fine chaff and insects.

- ✓ 'Threshing' is a technique for isolating bigger seeds from pods or plant matter. A plastic or calico bag is sealed and filled with seeds. The seeds are then separated into the bag using methods such as rolling, hand rubbing, whacking, and stomping with flat-soled shoes. It's a very relaxing method of stress relief! After the seeds and chaff have been separated, they are screened or winnowed for final cleaning.

**Processing Wet Seeds**

You must extract wet seeds from the flesh or pulp that surrounds them, then wash and dry subsequently. Scraping out the seeds, rinsing them, and drying them is pretty straightforward for most seeds. Other methods might be required. Let's take a look at some of them

- ✓ Fermenting cucumber and tomato seeds mimics the biological cycle of ripening and process of fermentation that takes place when ripe fruits fall to the ground and decay or are eaten by animals. Fermentation is required to cleanse tomato seeds and extract the germination-inhibiting gel that encapsulates each seed.

Mildews, molds, as well as other pathogens that may be found in eggplants and squash seeds can be killed by fermentation, but it is not required.

- ✓ Fill a jar halfway with boiling water and add the wet seeds and any pulp to ferment. Give it a thorough shake or mix many times a day. Allow the seeds to settle to the jar's bottom and separate from the flesh for a day or more. On the water's surface, you may observe bubbles, scum, or mold. After a day or two, take a few seeds to test if the pulpy covering has split. Check to see whether it works by rinsing. If the seed is clean, you can use a sieve to wash and dry the entire batch. If you ferment the seeds for longer than is necessary to clean them, they may germinate. If seeds sprout, they've been fermented for too long.

- ✓ Soaking makes the cleaning of seed easier by removing any pulpy remnants hanging onto the seed (e.g., melons and pumpkins). Soak seeds and pulp in a jar filled with water for nothing less than 8-12 hours to inhibit germination. Rinse well and pat dry.

- ✓ Decanting is the process of separating pulp and high-quality heavy seed from less viable lightweight seeds. Wash and grind the pulpy seed mixture first to split up large, lumpy particles. Load a container or big jar with seeds and pulp equal to at least ten times the amount of the pulp combination. Pour in a 4 parts water to a 1 part mixture of pulp. Shake and mix vigorously until the pulp disintegrates. Allow the heavy, fertile seed to sink to the bottom. Remove the floating pulp and fewer viable seeds from the topmost layer. Repeat until you have clear water and the heavy seed has settled to the bottom.

- ✓ Rinsing entails cleaning the seed with a screen, strainer, or colander, pressured water, and rubbing it with your palms before drying it. Fill a strainer halfway with wet seeds. Using your fingers, massage the pulp out from the strainer or colander while spraying it with water underneath running water. Strain it until the seeds are completely clean and no pulp remains. Rinsing through screens, on the other hand, causes the seeds to fall off the screens and into a bowl while the pulp stays on top.

- ✓ Drying. To absorb any leftover moisture, pat the strainer's base with a paper towel. After that, scatter seeds across any reflective surface (such as a ceramic plate, tray, or sheet of glass). Seeds will stick to any sort of paper. Place for a few days, or longer if necessary, in a warm, shady, dry location. When the seeds are completely dry, they should easily slip off the shining surface, ready for testing and storing.

**Final Drying of Seeds for Storage**

By maximizing airflow, dry all seeds as rapidly as possible. A fan that is set on low speed, air conditioning, or a food dehydrator that is nothing above 95°F (35°C) may help Distribute seeds over a fine layer of smooth, non-stick medium such as glass, ceramic plat, plastic tray, or wood. Paper towels and cardboard are good examples of materials that seeds attach to. To facilitate drying, rotate seeds as needed. Seeds will be harmed if the temperature rises above 95°F (35°C).

Test seeds to ascertain if they are well dried, which can be done via the test methods below;

- ✓ Hammer or bend test: Attempt to bend thin seeds, such as pumpkin seeds, or small, oblong seeds, such as lettuce seeds. They are dried well enough if they break rather than bend. Place large seeds (peas, beans, or maize) on a solid surface and pound them. If they're dried well enough, they should break vigorously. They will crush or mush if they are not well dried.

- ✓ Paper test: Overnight, place a piece of dry paper in your container and maintain a control piece away from the seeds. Compare the two the following day to determine whether the paper is still crispy or has softened due to moisture in the seeds.

- ✓ Al dente test: This determines how hard a seed is when bitten. If tooth marks can be made on it, then extra drying time is required.

Your seeds are now ready to be stored for a long time once they are well dried.

## Factors Affecting Seed Storage Longevity

The seed storage period is determined by three factors:

- ✓ Seed type
- ✓ Seed quality
- ✓ Storage condition

Seed storage longevity is affected by the following factors:

1. The Seed's Moisture Content — Even if seeds are completely dry, poor storage can cause them to absorb moisture. To avoid this from happening;

    To avoid being harmed by high moisture content,

    - ✓ Keep seeds in airtight containers (a securely closed metal bottle, a sealed thick plastic, or a tin can);
    - ✓ Keep seeds dry by incorporating desiccants or moisture-absorbing materials (e.g., silica gel, dry charcoal, toasted white rice, dry ash, lime) into the storage container; and,
    - ✓ Replace absorbents or desiccants every time the container is opened.

**Note:** Sun drying the seeds regularly will keep the moisture content of the seeds low.

2. Temperature — Whenever the storage temperature is low or cold (not freezing), the lifespan of vegetable seeds is extended. If you don't have access to a refrigerator or air conditioner, find a cool spot (near the river, underground, under trees, inside a clay jar). Make sure the seeds don't get moist.

As a rule of thumb:

When the moisture content of seeds is reduced by 1% and the storage temperature is reduced by 5°C, the life of the seeds becomes doubled.

Examples:

If a seed with a moisture level of 14% has a two-year storage life, it can be extended to four years if the moisture content is reduced to 13%.

If a seed's predicted life in a storage chamber with a 15°C temperature is 3 years, it can be extended to 6 years by lowering the storage temperature to 10°C.

When the seed's moisture content and storage temperature are both reduced, the seed's life span is extended.

| Moisture Content | Temperature | Storage Life | % Germination |
|---|---|---|---|
| 13% | 30°C | 1/2 year | 50% |
| 12% | 30°C | 1 year | 50% |
| 13% | 25°C | 1 year | 50% |
| 12% | 25°C | 2 years | 50% |
| 11% | 25°C | 4 years | 50% |
| 10% | 30°C | 4 years | 50% |

3. Insects — Seed's life span is reduced by storage weevils, fungus, and bacteria when stored. When the moisture content in the storage space reaches 10%, storage weevils begin to multiply. When the moisture content is 13%, fungi infestation becomes a concern. When the moisture content exceeds 20%, bacteria become an issue. During

storage, choose only pest-free seeds to avoid pest infection. Pest problems can also be avoided by keeping the seeds dry. Pest-control materials can also be employed to slow or stop pest growth and multiplication. These control methods are given below:

- ✓ Dry ash and charcoal — They absorb water and absorb it within the storage container. Weevils cannot grow or multiply in the presence of ash. For every kilo of seed, use half a kilo of ash. To keep the seeds from burning, use ash that has been cooled for at least 12 hours.

- ✓ Sand — Combine the sand with the seeds and fill the storage container completely to prevent the weevils from moving around.

- ✓ Cooking Oil — To inhibit the spread of weevils, some seeds can be combined with cooking oil. One teaspoon of oil per kilo of seeds is the suggested quantity.

- ✓ Lime — In addition to absorbing moisture, lime can also help to inhibit the proliferation of weevils. For every kilo of seeds, combine 15 teaspoons (approximately 50 grams) of lime.

✓ Leaves or seeds of various aromatic plants, dried and powdered — Weevils are sensitive to odorous plants, which prevents their multiplication and causes their death. The effect of the plants is determined by how they are prepared, how much is applied, and what kind of seed and weevils are used. Because some of these plants can have an effect on the seed, it's crucial to examine what's best for each type of seed. Also, be certain that the correct amount is used.

Aromatic Plants Examples

- Neem — The neem leaves or seeds should be dried in the sun and ground into a powder. For every kilo of seeds, combine 3-4 teaspoons (15-20 grams) of powdered neem seeds (twice the amount if using powdered leaves).

- Chili or hot pepper — Dried and powdered fruits are preferable to dried whole fruits. For

every kilo of seeds, combine 46 tablespoons (20-30 grams) of dry and powdered chili.
- Black pepper — For every kilo of seeds, combine 6 teaspoons (30 grams) of powdered black pepper (twice the amount if using powdered leaves).

Other plants to try include:

- 4 teaspoons (20 grams) powdered turmeric rhizome for every kilo of seeds

- For every kilo of seeds, combine 14 teaspoons (5-20 grams) of powdered mint leaves.

- 1-2 tablespoons (5-10 grams) of powdered yam bean seeds for every kilo of seeds

- 14 teaspoons (5-20 grams) powdered lagundi, mango, and tobacco leaves for every kilo of seeds

4. Other variables — Seeds can have a reduced storage life if they are overripe, come from plants that have been attacked by pests and diseases, or have been damaged when being processed.

**Labeling**

Label both the inside and exterior of the storage container, especially if you're storing several different kinds of seeds. The following details should be included on the label:

- ✓ the name of the seed
- ✓ the date it was harvested
- ✓ the date it was stored
- ✓ the date it was tested for germination; and
- ✓ the percentage of germination.

The plant and the seed's characteristics should also be captured if necessary.

**Testing Seed Quality**

You should always test for the quality of seed when selling seeds, buying seeds, sharing or giving seeds, storing seeds, and planting or sowing seeds.

Testing the quality of seeds is discussed under the following factors;

1. The Vigor of the Seed

It is necessary to determine the strength or vigor of seeds, particularly after they have been exposed to storage and planting conditions. Weak seeds planted in bad field conditions will die, or the plants that grow from them will be vulnerable to pests and diseases. As a result, yields will be minimal. Seeds that aren't strong will not last long in storage. Furthermore, even if a large number of seeds germinate, their germination and growth rates will be slow and uneven. Seed vigor, which is the speed and consistency of seed germination, should be determined at the same time you are ascertaining the percentage germination. Compare the speed, consistency and number of germination of the seeds you are testing to those with good seed quality.

Soaking the seeds in water can also be used to determine the vigor of the seeds. Weak seeds usually floats.

2. The Health of the Seed

Pests and diseases that can damage or kill seeds are not present in healthy seeds. They won't spread diseases nor infect other plants. Examine the seeds carefully if you don't have access to a microscope. Examine the seedcoat for imperfections or stains, molds, or holes caused by insects or insect's eggs. These seeds are not suitable for sowing because they may produce an epidemic or introduce a new pest or disease. Remove any diseased or contaminated seeds from the batch.

A disease can appear after the seeds have been sowed in some cases. Look for fungus or bacteria in developing seeds (symptoms of infection: seeds are watery, shiny and have bad smell). It'll also useful to know where the seeds were collected and what plant they came from, especially if you're looking for diseases spread by seeds.

By soaking the seeds in hot water (50°C) for 30 minutes, many fungus and bacteria can be destroyed. This approach, however, cannot kill all pests and diseases. Some seed health testing are best carried out in a lab. If you suspect your seeds are infected with pests or diseases, have them examined at the proper departments or agencies (example: Bureau of Plant Industry).

3. Seed Purity

When buying seeds, ensure you're buying the correct seeds or the ones as captured on the label. Only by thoroughly understanding the seeds' features can this be determined. Determine if the seeds contain impurities such as broken seeds, stones, dirt, leaves, or seeds from other plants, pests, and diseases. Seed quality suffers as a result of any of these pollutants. Before storing or sharing seeds with others, clean them if possible.

4. Seed Moisture Contents

Seeds that aren't oily (such ladyfinger and pechay) have a moisture content of 14 percent, while oily seeds have a moisture content of 12 percent (like soybean, peanut, yardlong bean and mungbean). Seed viability is reduced when moisture levels are high.

5. % Germination

The percentage of seed germination can be used to determine whether the seeds should be saved, planted, or discarded. This will also show how many seeds need to be sown in order to get the required number of plants. A water-absorbent substance is required. Use river sand or clean soil as a medium of germination for large seeds (before using, boiling water is normally poured over the soil to kill bacteria). For small seeds, the germination medium, such as paper (tissue paper, filter paper, etc.) or cloth (cheese cloth, etc.) can be used.

Arrange the seeds in the germination medium (not close together) and roll them out like a mat, or cover them with another layer of material. Do not overwater the seeds. Place the seeds in a box or plastic bag that allows air penetration, or stand it in a container with enough water to absorb upwards. Do not place the medium where ants and rats can reach and don't place in direct sunlight either.

Count the number of seedlings that are normal after several days (the ones that can continue to grow normally and those with normal leaves and roots).

Then calculate the % germination.

$$\% \text{ germination} = \frac{\text{number of normal seedlings}}{\text{total number of seed germinated}} \times 100$$

Example:

$$\% \text{ germination} = \frac{80 \text{ (number of normal seedlings)}}{100 \text{ (total number of seeds germinated)}} \times 100 = 80$$

The greater the number of seeds examined for percentage germination, the more precise the percentage germination will be. If possible, conduct multiple tests with 50 or more seeds. The number of seeds to plant can then be calculated as follows:

$$\text{number seeds to be planted} = \frac{\text{desired number of plants}}{\% \text{ germination}}$$

Example:

$$\text{number of seeds to be planted} = \frac{160 \text{ (desired number of plants)}}{80\% \text{ (percentage germination)}} = 200$$

## Abnormal Seeds

If the percentage of germination is less than 50%, don't store or plant the seeds. If saved, these seeds will likely yield poor seedlings and will degrade quickly. Some seeds do not germinate right away, not because they are dead, but because they are latent or do not absorb enough water (example: mungbean, winged bean). Furthermore, several temperate seeds (for example, pechay, carrot, and cabbage) absorb water but do not sprout rapidly, particularly when young or fresh.

Methods to open the seedcoat on hard-coated seeds are required (example: rubbing in sandpaper, use of nail cutter, or chipping with a knife). Take extreme precautions to avoid harming the embryo.

You can alternatively soak the seeds for 3-10 minutes in hot water (one part seed to ten parts water) or for 1-10 seconds in boiling water. The amount of time the seed needs to be soaked for is determined by the type of seed and its age. Seeds that are old, hard, and absorb water quickly should be soaked for less time than young, soft seeds that do not absorb water quickly. Seeds that are typically cultivated in cold climates can be kept in the cold for a few days in the germination medium before being transplanted to a planting area.

# A Short message from the Author:

Hey, I hope you are enjoying the book? I would love to hear your thoughts!

Many readers do not know how hard reviews are to come by and how much they help an author.

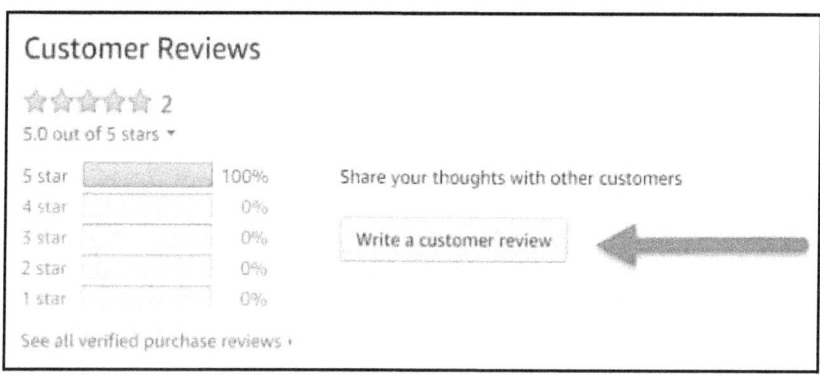

I would be incredibly grateful if you could take just 60 seconds to write a short review on Amazon, even if it is a few sentences!

\>> Click here to leave a quick review

Thanks for the time taken to share your thoughts!

# Chapter 4

# Saving Vegetable Seeds

## Common Vegetable Family To Save Seeds From

### Solanaceae: Tobacco or Nightshade Family

Potato, bell pepper, chili pepper, eggplant, tobacco, and tomato.

## Description:

- ✓ Possess alternate leaves
- ✓ It can be lobed, simple, or biternate
- ✓ It's most times pubescent
- ✓ It has a characteristic odor
- ✓ Its flower comes with connivent anthers (come to a point)
- ✓ It has 5 petals

- ✓ Its fruit is a berry
- ✓ Grown as annuals

**Characteristics:**

- ✓ Has several common pests and diseases, such as tobacco mosaic, nematodes, verticillium, and fusarium fungus
- ✓ Works well with moist, rich soil with plenty of organic matter

**Fabaceae (Leguminosae): Bean or Pea Family**

Fava beans Peas, peanuts, green/string beans, peas, hyacinth bean, cowpea.

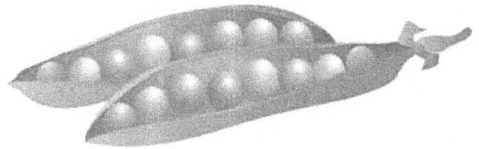

**Description:**

- ✓ It has compound, alternate leaves, either pinnate or trifoliate
- ✓ It's fruit is a legume
- ✓ It splits open, with its seeds on one side

**Characteristics:**

- ✓ It has high protein seeds and leaves
- ✓ It uses little quantity of well-rotted compost
- ✓ Has a day-long flowering beans

**Cucurbitaceae: Gourd Family**

Luffa, watermelon, winter squash, melons, gourds, cucumbers, zucchini

**Description:**

- ✓ It is mostly annuals
- ✓ It's most times bristly haired
- ✓ It has tendrils
- ✓ It has simple, large, alternate, and palmately lobed leaves.
- ✓ Its flowers are mostly unisexual

**Characteristics:**

- ✓ Grows very fast
- ✓ Requires being kept moist, not wet
- ✓ Use several composts
- ✓ Except it is below 3 weeks old, transplanting doesn't work well

- ✓ It grows on trellis
- ✓ It is susceptible to blights and mildews

## Malvaceae: Mallow or Hibiscus Family

Okra, cotton, hibiscus, roselle

## Description:

- ✓ It has veined or palmately lobed leaves
- ✓ Mostly hairy
- ✓ Its fruit capsules are dehiscing
- ✓ Has several carpels
- ✓ It has large flowers with staminate spray in the middle
- ✓ Its stamens are unified by filaments in the tube around the pistil.

## Characteristics:

- ✓ It requires sun and heat
- ✓ It is drought tolerant

- ✓ It doesn't do well when transplanted
- ✓ It is susceptible to flea beetles
- ✓ It's sometimes aphids

## Alliaceae, Liliaceae or Amaryillidaceae: Onion Family

Chive leek, onion, garlic

### Description:

- ✓ They are monocots in nature
- ✓ Their base push up the leaves
- ✓ Its leaves are long and thin
- ✓ It preserves nourishment in the underground shoots (swollen bulbs)
- ✓ It has a long life cycle, majorly biennial or perennial

### Characteristics:

- ✓ Its leaves require cool weather, while its bulb requires hot and dry weather
- ✓ Its roots are very shallow
- ✓ It bolts if the flower stems are not taken out
- ✓ Works well in loamy soils
- ✓ Requires thinning and weeding

- ✓ It requires adequate water

**Poaceae (Gramineae): Grasses or Grains Family**

Sugar cane, rice, lemongrass, corn, wheat

**Description:**

- ✓ They are monocots in nature
- ✓ Its leaves are strap-shaped with sheaths
- ✓ Its roots are fibrous in nature either, rhizomes or stolons.
- ✓ It has a large family and are the most critical economic crops.
- ✓ It has simple, alternate leaves
- ✓ They are tiny, pollinated by wind, and mostly unisexual flowers

**Characteristics:**

- ✓ They are heavy feeders and require lots of fertilizer or organic matter

- ✓ Organic matter are planted in the soil through its fibrous roots
- ✓ To promote pollination, plant in blocks.
- ✓ Some are perennial, most are annuals.

**Brassicaceae (Cruciferae): Mustard Family**

Cauliflower radish, cabbage, mustard, Pak choi, broccoli, kale.

**Description:**

- ✓ It has simple, alternate leaves with hairs or waxy cuticles.
- ✓ They are mostly biennial
- ✓ Its plants possess a characteristic sulfuric odor

**Characteristics:**

- ✓ It is mostly a cool-season crop

- ✓ It can utilize a small amount of water due to its waxy cuticle
- ✓ Its roots are shallow
- ✓ It performs poorly in acid soil; add lots of organic matter to mitigate the pH of the soil
- ✓ Its leaves are eaten by cabbage moth larvae. So ensure to tie it closed

## Chenopodiaceae: Goosefoot Family

Chard, beet, spinach

## Description:

- ✓ They can be either annual or biennial (beet)
- ✓ It has simple, large, alternate leaves with a continuous leaf surface.
- ✓ They are tiny with green flowers and are easily confused with amaranths

## Characteristics:

- ✓ They are well-rooted deeply in the soil (up to 3 meters)
- ✓ It breaks up the soil and recycles nutrients
- ✓ They are cool-season vegetables

- ✓ The soil on which it is planted need to be drained well enough with well-rotted compost
- ✓ They don't perform well in acidic soil
- ✓ It requires to be deeply watered

## Amaranthaceae: Pigweed Or Amaranth Family

Amaranths, celosias

## Description:

- ✓ Its leaves are simple, alternate, or opposite
- ✓ Its flowers are often pubescent, usually racemes or spikes

## Characteristics:

- ✓ They are drought-tolerant
- ✓ They require lots of sun
- ✓ Their harvest period takes time
- ✓ Likes manure
- ✓ To maintain the production of leaves, simply pinch off their flowers

## Apiaceae (Umbelliferae): Parsley Family

Carrot, coriander, fennel, parsley, celery

**Description:**

- ✓ They are mostly cool-season crops
- ✓ It requires water
- ✓ It requires either a sandy or loamy, but well-drained soil (with no heavy clay)
- ✓ It doesn't require fresh manure; you can simply add ashes or rock phosphate
- ✓ They are quite slow when it comes to seed germination
- ✓ They easily cross-pollinate

**Lamiaceae (Labiatae): Mint Family**

Oregano mints, rosemary, thyme, basil, sage

**Description:**

- ✓ They can serve as aromatic herbs
- ✓ Most are perennial in nature
- ✓ They act as shrubs sometimes
- ✓ They have four-sided stems
- ✓ Their leaves are opposite or whorled
- ✓ Their flowers are bilabiate in nature

**Characteristics:**

- ✓ They are drought-tolerant
- ✓ They can accommodate poor soils
- ✓ Their roots are invasive and extensive
- ✓ They have a large and thick canopy

**Saving Seeds Quick Guide of Common Vegetables**

Below is a quick rundown on what you should be aware of when saving seeds from common vegetables.

Bear in mind to read this section in tandem with the previously covered chapters.

## Beans

- ✓ Bean flowers nearly never cross-pollinate since they are self-pollinating
- ✓ Plant different varieties of beans 10 feet apart with caution
- ✓ Seeds from the largest, earliest maturing, and best-tasting plants should be saved
- ✓ Allow seed pods to dry completely before crushing them in a sack
- ✓ Separate the seed from the pods

## Beets

- ✓ Seed saving of beets are biennial
- ✓ Because beet varieties cross-pollinate, they must be kept apart from other beets, 0.5 miles away (2,600 feet)
- ✓ Pull up the beet plant in the fall, trim the leaves to 2", and store in a root cellar over the winter
- ✓ At 32-40° F, roots can be stored for 4-6 months
- ✓ Replant seeds in the spring and harvest the heads of the seed when they are dry

## Broccoli
- ✓ Seed saving of beets are biennial
- ✓ Isolate broccoli from all other Brassica oleracea plants by 1 mile (5,200 ft).
- ✓ Remove plants from the soil in the fall and pot them in sand.
- ✓ Plants should be stored between 32 and 40° F
- ✓ Early in the spring, transplant outside, allowing to bolt.
- ✓ When the seed pods are dry, harvest them and clean them by hand.

## Brussel Sprouts
- ✓ Seed saving of Brussel sprouts are biennial
- ✓ Isolate Brussel sprouts from all other Brassica oleracea plants by 1 mile (5,200 feet)
- ✓ Remove plants from the soil in the fall and pot them in sand.
- ✓ Plants should be stored between 32 and 40° F
- ✓ Early in the spring, transplant outside, allowing to bolt
- ✓ When the seed pods are dry, harvest them and clean them by hand

## Cabbage
- ✓ Seed saving of cabbage are biennial

- ✓ Isolate cabbage from all other Brassica oleracea plants by 1 mile (5,200 feet)
- ✓ Remove plants from the soil in the fall and pot them in sand.
- ✓ Plants should be stored between 32 and 40° F
- ✓ Early in the spring, transplant outside, allowing to bolt
- ✓ When the seed pods are dry, harvest them and clean them by hand

## Carrot

- ✓ Seed saving of carrot are biennial
- ✓ Isolate carrot from all other varieties to prevent cross-pollination by 1 mile (5,200 feet)
- ✓ Harvest carrot roots in the fall, trim leaves to 1 inch and store in a root cellar over the winter
- ✓ At 32-40° F, roots can be stored for 4-6 months
- ✓ Replant seeds in the spring and harvest the heads of the seed when they are dry

## Cauliflower

- ✓ Seed saving of cauliflower are biennial
- ✓ Isolate cauliflower from all other Brassica oleracea plants by 1 mile (5,200 feet)
- ✓ Plants should be stored between 32 and 40° F

- ✓ Remove plants from the soil in the fall and pot them in sand.
- ✓ Early in the spring, transplant outside, allowing to bolt
- ✓ When the seed pods are dry, harvest them and clean them by hand

## Corn

- ✓ Within a mile (5,200 feet) of each other, all corn varieties will cross-pollinate. If you grow varieties closer than this stipulate distance, then hand pollinate
- ✓ Allow ears to dry on the stem for a few days before harvesting and shelling the seeds. Clear off any debris.

## Cucumbers

- ✓ Within 0.25 miles (1,300 feet) of each other, all cucumber varieties will cross-pollinate
- ✓ When cucumbers are ready to be harvested, they should be large with yellow coloration.
- ✓ Cut lengthwise, scoop out seeds, wash, and dry.
- ✓ When seeds break instead of bending, it means they are dry.

## Eggplant

- ✓ Within 0.25 miles (1,300 feet) of each other, all eggplant varieties will cross-pollinate
- ✓ Allow the fruits to grow way beyond maturity before harvesting the seeds
- ✓ Scoop out seeds, wash, and dry
- ✓ When seeds break instead of bending, it means they are dry.

## Lettuce

- ✓ Lettuce cross-pollinate infrequently, but it should be kept 15" away from other varieties when its seeds are to be harvested.
- ✓ Repeated harvesting over a 2-3 week period may be required to gather most seeds. The dried seed should be removed from the stalk.

## Melon

- ✓ Within 0.25 miles (1,300 feet) of each other, all melon varieties (cantaloupe, muskmelons, and honeydews) will cross-pollinate
- ✓ Scoop out seeds, wash, and dry
- ✓ When seeds break instead of bending, it means they are dry

## Okra

- ✓ All okra cultivars will cross-pollinate within a mile (5,200 ft) of each other.
- ✓ Okra pods will dry off and become brown on the plant.
- ✓ When the first pod starts to splits open, it's time to harvest

## Onions

- ✓ Seed saving of onions are biennial
- ✓ All onion cultivars will cross-pollinate within a mile (5,200 ft) of each other
- ✓ Harvest only large, consistent onions in the fall and preserve over the winter in a root cellar
- ✓ At 32-40° F, roots can be stored for 3-6 months
- ✓ In the spring, replant bulbs and harvest seed heads once dry

## Peas

- ✓ Peas cross-pollinate infrequently; however, keep them from other cultivars at about 50-inches apart
- ✓ Before you harvest, allow the pods on the plant to become brown and dry. Break the pods away from the beans, then remove the pods

## Peppers
- ✓ Within 200 ft (sweet pepper) and 800 ft (hot pepper) of each other, varieties of all pepper will cross-pollinate
- ✓ Ripe and healthy peppers should be harvested
- ✓ Remove the seeds from the core and allow them to dry. When seeds snap rather than bend, it means they are dry

## Pumpkins
- ✓ All pumpkins cultivars will cross-pollinate within 0.25 miles (1,300 ft) of each other
- ✓ Ripe and healthy pumpkins should be harvested. Extract the seeds from within. Wash and dry the seeds. When seeds snap rather than bend, it means they are dry

## Radish
- ✓ All radish cultivars will cross-pollinate within 0.5 miles (2,600 ft) of each other
- ✓ Radish seed stalks can reach a height of 3 feet. Early bolting should be discarded because it is undesirable

- ✓ Harvest the stalks of the seed when both the stalk and pods become dry. You can separate the seeds with your hand

## Spinach

- ✓ All spinach cultivars will cross-pollinate within 0.5 miles (2,600 ft) of each other
- ✓ When the seeds are totally dried on the plant, harvest them. Seeds can be very sharp, so be cautious

## Squash

- ✓ All squash cultivars will cross-pollinate within 0.25 miles (1,300 ft) of each other
- ✓ Allow the fruits to stay for about 2-3 months after it has matured before harvesting the seed.
- ✓ Scoop out the seeds, wash, and dry them. When seeds snap rather than bend, it means they are dry

## Tomatoes

- ✓ Cross-pollination between tomato varieties is rare, except for potato leaf varieties, which should be kept 25" apart
- ✓ 1 week after prime picking, select the tomatoes with the most desired characteristics

- ✓ Fill a jar with seeds and set aside for fermentation. Fill the jar with the same amount of water as the seeds. Allow it to ferment for 3-4 days or until mild mold starts to form
- ✓ The bottom seeds are healthy and ready to dry

# Chapter 5

## Saving Flower Seeds

**Saving Seeds From Common Flowers**

# Calendula

From early summer till frost, calendula (Calendula officinalis) grown from seed produces a stunning display of pale yellow to deep orange blossoms. Sun-loving plants are typically low and compact, with lovely double flowers that range in size from 2-1/2 to 4 inches in diameter. Sow straight in the garden or start in flats for early season flowering. In patio pots or mixed borders, this plant is stunning.

## Calendula Quick Guide: Planting, Growing, and Caring

- ✓ Get bright, sassy orange and yellow flowers
- ✓ Requires full sun to partial shade
- ✓ It takes about 45-60 days to mature from seed to flower
- ✓ Typically 18-24 inches tall
- ✓ In all directions, the spacing should be between 24 and 36 inches.
- ✓ Simple planting indoors (start 6-8 wks before the last frost) or outdoors (sow after the last frost)
- ✓ It provides full sun and potting soil or compost-rich soil
- ✓ Bloom throughout the season; deadhead and fertilize to encourage more blooms
- ✓ They're wonderful for companion planting with marigolds because they'll help repel insects

**Preparing the Site**

Plants adores full sun, but partial shade will suffice in warmer climates. Calendula thrives in big containers filled with organic potting soil or in garden beds. To improve soil conditions, work a shovelful or two of well-aged compost or manure into the ground before sowing in the beds.

## Planting Instructions

Calendula is a cool-weather plant which can be grown inside under artificial light 6-8 weeks just before the frost or sown outside after the last frost. It takes 5-15 days for seeds to germinate. Throughout the growing season, water thoroughly and apply a liquid bloom fertilizer on a regular basis to develop huge, gorgeous blossoms. To lengthen the duration of the blooming period, pinch off "spent flowers" regularly. Mulch to keep roots cool, avoid weeds, and save moisture.

## Insect and Disease Issues

Calendula isn't usually affected by insects or disease. In fact, many insect pests may be deterred by the blossom, making it an excellent companion plant for vegetable gardens – for additional protection from insects, plant marigolds around chard, tomatoes, and carrots.

**Instructions for Seed Saving**

Calendula, like zinnias and marigolds, produces a large amount of seed. Cut the blooms off when they're dry and hang them upside down in bunches. The seeds are retained in the heads, which can be gently crushed and winnowed to separate the chaff of the seed from the seeds once it is dry and crispy.

**Zinnia**

Zinnias are colorful flowers that are easy to grow from seed and come in a wide variety of colors and sizes. Zinnias are a good choice if you're looking for a flower with low-maintenance to brighten up your garden beds. Their vibrantly colored, often intricately stacked blossoms last well into the summer, making them a popular choice. Larger zinnia cultivars are popular in cut flower arrangements and can also be used to liven up annual or mixed border plantings. Smaller kinds are ideal for pots, window boxes, and front-of-the-garden planting.

Songbirds, butterflies, and pollinators are all attracted to vibrant blossoms. Plant a rainbow of hues in your flower gardens and watch them spring to life. Zinnias are linked to daisies, cosmos, marigolds, and sunflowers because they are part of the aster family.

**Zinnia Quick Guide: Planting, Growing, and Caring**

- ✓ One of the easiest and most colorful annuals
- ✓ Beneficial insects, butterflies, and birds are attracted to it
- ✓ Start seeds 6-8 wks indoors before the last frost date or outdoor after the last frost date

- ✓ Full and direct sunlight is required; fertilize once a month
- ✓ Its prone to pests such as black spot, powdery mildew, and rust
- ✓ Can accept an average soil but does well when you add organic matter
- ✓ It takes about 60-75 days to mature from seed to flower
- ✓ It has a height of about 18-24 inches
- ✓ The recommended spacing in all directions should be about 6-12 inches apart

**Preparing the Site**

Zinnias are a warm-weather annual flower that thrives in direct sunlight and well-drained soil. They're easy to grow and can withstand medium to slightly poor soils. Garden beds prepared with significant volumes of organic compost or well-aged animal manure will greatly boost plant health.

## Planting Instructions

For transplanting outside, start zinnia seeds inside about 6-8 wks before the last frost date. Sow seeds straight into planting spaces in warmer climates and lightly cover with dirt. After the seeds have grown, vigorously water them and thin them out to 6-12 inches apart. Flowers, once established, will survive in a variety of conditions, even if they are left unattended.

Once the plants start flowering, fertilize monthly using an organic bloom-boosting fertilizer. To lengthen the blooming season, pinch off the "spent blooms." Mulch to conserve moisture, reduce weeds, and improve the appearance of your garden. Severe cold or freeze will kill zinnias.

## Insect and Disease Issues

Pest infestations such as black spots, rust, and powdery mildew can affect zinnia plants. If you detect any symptoms of these, we recommend that you do the following:

- ✓ If at all possible, avoid watering from above (use soaker hoses or drip irrigation)
- ✓ Plants should be properly spaced to facilitate air circulation.
- ✓ To avoid future infection, use copper spray or sulfur dust.

**Instructions for Seed Saving**

Zinnias fertilize each other. To save pristine seed, plant one type at a given period or separate varieties by ¼ mile. When the blossoms turn brown and dry, it's time to gather the seeds. The seeds are kept in the exact center of the container. When the heads are completely dry, carefully smash them with your hands and carefully winnow off the chaff.

**Cosmos**

Cosmos flowers are a great choice for borders and backgrounds because of their tall stalks, eye-catching colors, and fern-like leaves. Cosmos is a personal fave. Cosmos lends delicate elegance to your summer gardens, especially when planted in informal beds or mixed borders. Flowers are available in vibrant reds and oranges, as well as gentler crimsons and creams. Cut flowers as soon as they blossom and place them in cold water for proper arrangements. Containers are ideal for shorter varieties.

Be prepared for this half-hardy annual to grow to a height of 2-5 feet in the garden.

## Cosmos Quick Guide: Planting, Growing, and Caring

- ✓ White, yellow, red, pink, and purple are just a few of the many colors available in cosmos flowers
- ✓ Their height ranges anywhere from 3-5 feet tall depending on the variety
- ✓ It's easy to grow cosmos in full to partial shade sunlight and in rich soil
- ✓ It's ideal for climates that are dry
- ✓ Sow seed outdoors after the last frost or 4-5 wks indoors before the last frost
- ✓ Beneficial insects love it because it blooms all year.
- ✓ It takes about 65-90 days to mature from seed to flower
- ✓ In all directions, space the plants 12-8 inches apart

### Preparing the Site

Cosmos thrive on rich, fast-draining soil and plenty of sunlight. They are, nevertheless, hardy and can survive a wide range of soil conditions as well as partial shade. It only necessitates a reasonable amount of water and little attention. If at all possible, provide wind protection. Suitable for xeriscapes and water-conserving gardening.

**Planting Instructions**

Sow flower seeds for annuals. Sow 1/8 inch deep outdoors after the last frost, or indoors, 4-5 weeks before the last frost. In about 3-10 days, germination of the seeds will occur. Cosmos plants do not feed alot. Plants that receive lots of fertilizer will create too much leaf growth at the price of blossom output. To lengthen the blossoming season, support a few of the taller varieties by pinching off the "spent blooms." After the first heavy frost in the fall, remove and discard the plants.

Grow cosmos as a border surrounding vegetable crops to lure beneficial insects like bees and butterflies.

**Insect and Disease Issues**

There aren't many pest problems with cosmos. Aphids, on the other hand, can appear virtually overnight. To limit the number of these soft-bodied sucking insects, keep an eye on them and spray them with a powerful stream of water. If a speedy knock-down is necessary, use Safer® Soap.

Fungal diseases such as gray mold and powdery mildew, which can disorient plants if severe, can also affect foliage and blooms. To decrease and avoid common plant diseases, do the following;

- ✓ If at all possible, avoid watering from above (use soaker hoses or drip irrigation)
- ✓ Plants should be properly spaced to facilitate air circulation
- ✓ To avoid further infection, use organic fungicides

**Instructions for Seed Saving**

Plants reproduce by self-seeding. If you want to conserve the seed, remember that the flowers may not always come true to type; fancy variants frequently revert to the single-flower form.

**Morning Glory**

Annual morning glory (Ipomoea) vines, with their huge, trumpet-shaped flowers, are a true old-fashioned beauty and are easy to cultivate from seed.

This is a wonderful vintage gem! Morning glory is a popular flower among home flower growers because of its brilliant colors, which include purples, reds, pinks, and blues. This robust vining plant (up to 15 feet tall) is frequently found covering country fences, where its lovely blossoms greet you as the sun rises. Give these hardy annuals some love and watch them grow as they cover walls, privacy screens, and lattice. Dwarf varieties are extremely distinctive, with their multi-colored blooms! Put them in containers against a trellis and see what happens. Because these climbing beauties self-seed, they'll most likely return year after year in the same location. Their big fragrant flowers attract birds and bees.

## Morning Glory Quick Guide: Planting, Growing, and Caring

- ✓ The colors are vibrant purple, pink, red, and blue
- ✓ They are self-seeding annual that can reach a height of 6-18 feet if maintained
- ✓ After the last frost, direct seed, but the seed must be prepared for optimal results (see above)
- ✓ Direct and full sunlight and consistent moisture are required.
- ✓ It blooms from late summer to early autumn.
- ✓ It takes about 75-110 days to mature from seed to flower

- ✓ In all directions, space the flowers 4-6 inches apart

## Preparing the Site

Choose a location that attracts lots of sun and has wet, well-drained soil. Before planting, work organic compost or well-aged animal manure into the soil to assist plants to retain moisture and avoid wilting during the day.

## Planting Instructions

Morning glory is a simple seedling to nurture. After the last frost, plant outdoors 1/2 inch deep and maintain wet until germination. In 5 to 21 days, the seeds will germinate. For better results, nick the seeds and soak them in water for 24 hours before planting. Seedlings should be spaced 4-6 inches apart. Assist the young plants in climbing by providing support.

If you're having difficulties getting morning glory seeds to germinate, make sure they're planted in full light and don't let them dry out until they're established. During the growing season, apply an organic bloom fertilizer two or three times.

**Insect and Disease Issues**

Morning glory is attacked by several garden pests, including aphids and leafminer. Keep a watchful eye on things and use the following common sense, non-toxic pest management methods;

- ✓ To eliminate alternate hosts, remove weeds and other garden waste
- ✓ Severely contaminated plants should be bagged and discarded in the garbage
- ✓ Beneficial insects (such as ladybugs and lacewings) that are commercially accessible should be released to attack and remove insect pests. Use neem oil or another organic insecticide to spot-treat pest problem areas

Rust and Fusarium wilt are two fungal diseases that can affect foliage and flowers. To reduce the spread of these plant diseases, take the following steps;

- ✓ If at all possible, avoid watering from above (use soaker hoses or drip irrigation)
- ✓ Plants should be properly spaced to facilitate air circulation
- ✓ To avoid future infection, use copper or sulfur sprays
- ✓ Remove and do away with infected plants if issues persist

**Instructions for Seed Saving**

Morning glories will pollinate each other. To save prestine seed or isolate varieties by ¼ mile, plant only one variety at a given period. When the seed capsules are entirely dry and brown, the seeds are ready to harvest.

**Nasturtium**

Nasturtiums (Tropaeolum) spread eye-catching colors just where you need them, and they're quick and easy to grow. This quick-growing, colorful annual that self-seeds should be included in your garden and hanging baskets. Nasturtium is grown from seeds and cuttings by home gardeners for its bright, showy flowers and lovely trailing vines. Its gorgeous petals can also be used to liven up salads and pastas and they're delicious!

Ground covers, window boxes, walls, and trellised pots benefit from fragrant plants with vivid green leaves and orange, red, and yellow blooms. Nasturtiums are a great flower for kids to interact with since they grow quickly and have large seeds that are easy to handle with small hands. This resilient, carefree annual needs a lot of space to spread its wings – up to 10 feet, depending on the type.

## Nasturtiums Quick Guide: Planting, Growing, and Caring

- ✓ Yellow, orange, and deep red are some of the sun-loving colors that bloom
- ✓ When planted after the last frost, it is easy to grow from seed
- ✓ It requires full sunlight to partial shade and grows quickly
- ✓ It almost flourishes on neglect; no fertilizer is required; water on a regular basis
- ✓ Blooms during the entire season
- ✓ It takes about 55-70 days to mature from seed to flower
- ✓ It has a height of about 12-18 inches
- ✓ Space them about 8-2 inches apart in all directions

## Preparing the Site

Nasturtiums uses full sunlight and moist soil but will grow in partial shade as well. In warmer regions, plant in dappled shade and add a shovelful or two of organic matter (such as manure or well-aged animal dung) to the soil. This increases drainage and keeps roots cool by conditioning the soil

## Planting Instructions

Sow outside one week after the last frost, ¼ inch below the soil surface. In about 7-12 days, nasturtium seeds will start germinating and growing rapidly. During the planting season, plants don't need fertilizer. In fact, they appear to flourish in arid conditions. To lengthen the blossoming season, support a few of the taller climbing cultivars and pinching off the "spent blooms."

## Insect and Disease Issues

Common garden pests on nasturtiums include aphids, slugs, whiteflies, and flea beetles. Keep an eye on things and use insecticidal soap with pyrethrin or **diatomaceous earth** as needed. Several diseases affect foliage and flowers, including bacterial leaf spot and aster yellows, which disorient leaves and blooms.

To reduce plant fungal infections, do the following:

- ✓ If at all possible, avoid watering from above (use soaker hoses or drip irrigation)
- ✓ Plants should be properly spaced to facilitate air circulation
- ✓ To avoid future infection, use copper spray or sulfur dust

**Instructions for Seed Saving**

Nasturtiums will pollinate each other. To save pristine seed or isolate variants by ½ mile, plant only one type at a given period. Underneath the blooms, seeds form in pods containing roughly 2-3 big seeds. Because pod tend to rupture, it's a good idea to wrap an old sheet of newspaper across the plants. It's also possible to pick the seedpods a little early.

**Sunflower**

Sunflowers (Helianthus annuus) are a midsummer garden classic that are both tasty and decorative. A kid's favorite! Sunflowers are grown from seed by home flower growers for their vibrant colors, big blooms, and brilliant golden heads. They come in a variety of sizes, from miniatures for edging to over 10 feet tall with 2-foot diameter blooms, and are easy to start indoors. The blossoms are large and rich in color, ranging from typical yellow and orange to cream and brown. Sunflower seeds germinate quickly and can grow into little to large plants. Best of all, they produce a large number of seeds at the end of the season, making them an excellent plant for kids.

Sunflowers should be planted in full sun and rich soil on the north side of the garden to avoid shading other plants.

## Sunflowers Quick Guide: Planting, Growing, and Caring

- ✓ Choose between dwarf and gigantic varieties of yellow, red, and orange colors
- ✓ Direct seeding is best suggested once the danger of frost has passed
- ✓ Direct and full sunlight is required, as well as average to rich soil that can sustain vigorous roots
- ✓ When the blooms have stopped, allow to dry before saving seeds or leaving in the garden to feed birds
- ✓ They are scarely disturbed by pests and diseases
- ✓ From seed to flower, it takes 60-95 days
- ✓ It has a height of about 2-10 feet

- ✓ Space the flowers about 4-12 inches away in all directions

**Preparing the Site**

Sunflowers should be planted in full sun and rich soil on the north side of the garden to avoid shading other plants. Sunflowers should not be planted in sandy soil because they require a strong base to support their tall, top-heavy plants.

**Planting Instructions**

Sow 4 to 12 inches apart when all danger of frost has passed, with 1/2 inch of soil covering them. After you've finished sowing outside, keep an eye out for squirrels and birds that like to steal the newly planted seeds to augment their nutrition. Use CowPots or newspaper pots to start seedlings indoors and then plant them immediately in the garden.

Plants that are well-established and healthy will continue to grow even if they are left alone. When plants become top heavy, water to keep the soil slightly damp and provide support. To attract birds to your yard, leave mature flower heads on the plants.

You can also plant sunflowers in a circle to form a children's sunflower house, or in a row to make a quiet, beautiful sunflower hedge.

**Insect and Disease Issues**

Sunflowers aren't usually disturbed by insects and disease.

**Instructions for Seed Saving**

To ensure pure seed, separate sunflowers by 1/2 mile. When the heads have completely filled out, lost all of their petals, and the backs have begun to turn brown, it's time to harvest them. Allow to dry off in a safe location before shelling by hand.

## Marigold

Marigolds (Tagetes erecta), which are easy to cultivate and can be grown from seed, produce a brilliant splash of color throughout the summer. Marigolds are a favorite with gardeners from coast to coast! Marigolds are one of the most straightforward — and attractive — annuals to grow. Compact blooms in a range of colors from mild yellow to deep orange and rust look great in pots, baskets, and borders or simply sprinkled over the yard. This rapid germinator has a spicy perfume and provides a flash of color throughout the summer. It's also lovely in dried floral arrangements!

Marigolds are tolerant of a large variety of soil and climatic conditions, although they thrive in the heat.

This bright garden favorite comes in a large variety of sizes, from small to massive. To deter insect pests, plant marigolds in and around vegetable plants. They are hardy annuals that grow to be 10-18 inches tall.

## Marigold Quick Guide: Planting, Growing, and Caring

- ✓ The most frequent color is bright yellow, but there are also light yellow and deep orange varieties
- ✓ After the last frost, plant seedlings outside, or sow seeds inside 6-8 wks before the last frost.
- ✓ Choose a location that will provide direct, full sunlight and one whose soil is modified with compost
- ✓ Water on a regular basis and protect from frost
- ✓ An annual that flowers for the entire season
- ✓ It grows into a height of about 6-18 inches
- ✓ It takes about 50-80 days for it to mature from seed to flower

- ✓ Space the flowers about 8-18 inches away in all directions

**Preparing the Site**

Marigolds aren't picky and can thrive in a variety of environments. These plants, on the other hand, will grow in rich, well-drained soil with lots of sunlight. A considerable amount of organic compost or well-aged dung should be mixed into the garden before sowing. This will substantially increase the health of the flowers. Maintain a moist soil, but not damp.

**Planting Instructions**

Directly plant marigold seed into the soil, then use a thin layer of dirt (approximately 1/8 inch deep) to cover it up. Thoroughly wet the area. Thin seedlings to 8-18 inches apart after they have grown. You can also start marigolds under grow lights indoors and transplanted outside 6-8 wks before the last frost date. Even if left unchecked, marigolds will continue to thrive once planted and healthy. Keep the soil moist by watering. Once the plants have begun to flower, provide with nutrients and a bud and bloom booster on a monthly basis. To lengthen the blossoming season, pinch off the "spent flowers." Mulch to keep weeds at bay, retain moisture, and improve the look of your garden. A strong cold or ice will kill marigolds.

**Insect and Disease Issues**

Marigolds have few insect and pest concerns. In fact, the blooms can be used to dissuade and repel cabbage moths by planting them around cabbage and broccoli plants. Keep a watch out for slugs, which may completely destroy your plants in a matter of hours. If any damage is discovered, treat with Sluggo® Bait or diatomaceous earth. To control soft-bodied pests such as aphids and spider mites, spray them with a strong stream of water or spot treat strongly affected areas with Safer's® Soap.

**Instructions for Seed Saving**

Marigolds, like zinnias and calendulas, yield a large amount of seed. Cut the blooms off when they're dry and hang them upside down in bunches. Once the seeds are dry and crispy, they are retained in the heads and can be crushed and winnowed off the chaff of the seed.

**Sweet Pea**

Sweet peas (Lathyrus odoratus), with their distinctive shape and sweet fragrance, thrive in rich soil and moderate temperatures. Sweet pea is a fantastic climber that thrives on fences and trellises. Sweet peas are grown for their delicious scent and award-winning flowers by home flower gardeners. They offer gentle, diverse colors to bouquets and trellised borders. They are easy to start from seed. They don't tolerate heat and will stop flowering if it gets too hot, so plant early and mulch well to keep the roots cool.   This hardy annual is one of the earliest seeds to get into the ground, around 4-6 weeks before the last frost date. There are a few perennial sweet pea varieties available, but they don't have any scent and only come in whites and pinks.

**Sweet Peas Quick Guide: Planting, Growing, and Caring**

- ✓ Choose from a variety of colors, including pink, blue, purple, red, and others
- ✓ Direct seed as soon as you can work the soil in the early spring
- ✓ Plant in direct, full sunlight with organic or compost matter added to the soil

- ✓ Aphids, snails, and powdery mildew are among the pests and diseases that affect sweat peas
- ✓ Regularly water the soil; in hot weather, the plants will have a slow growth
- ✓ From seed to flower, it takes 55-75 days
- ✓ Its height ranges from about 48-72 inches
- ✓ In all directions, space the flowers 4-6 inches apart

## Preparing the Site

Sweet peas prefer a rich, well-drained soil, although they may grow in a variety of environments. To increase germination, soak seeds before planting. Sow seeds straight into the soil, 4-6 inches apart, and cover with 1/2 inch of dirt.

## Planting Instructions

Early in the spring, sow sweet pea seeds immediately the soil can be cultivated. Because seed casings are hard, soak them overnight for the best germination results. Plants want bright sunlight and cool temperatures.

During periods of drought, water flowers regularly to keep them blooming. Use an organic flower fertilizer formulated for numerous blooms several times in the gardening season. The majority of vining sweet peas require trellis support to climb, so offer one. Cut the flowers off the vines once they begin to bloom and bring them inside to enjoy. The more flowers you cut, the more the flowers will grow.

Flower production will decrease as the temperature warms. Chop the foliage and turn it into the existing soil as a free source of organic nitrogen— this should be done when when flower production slows and the vines begin to dry. Sweet peas, while being an annual, will reseed and bloom again the following spring.

**Insect and Disease Issues**

Aphids and slugs harm the foliage and blooms of sweet peas occasionally. If aphids are found, keep an eye on them and use diatomaceous earth or another OMRI-listed pesticide. Slug damage is visible as large irregular holes in the foliage and partially devoured seedlings. To kill slugs and snails without harming people, pets, or wildlife, scatter Sluggo®, an organic iron phosphate bait, around plants. Mildew and plant diseases thrive in rainy, chilly conditions. If you observe wilting, stains, or rotting tissue, you should do the following:

- ✓ If at all possible, avoid watering from above (use soaker hoses or drip irrigation)
- ✓ Plants should be properly spaced to facilitate air circulation
- ✓ To avoid future infection, use copper spray or sulfur dust

Ladybugs and green lacewings are attracted to sweet peas. To attract these pest-eating beneficial insects, plant them in and around your food gardens

**Instructions for Seed Saving**

To maintain ultimate purity, plants should be separated by 25 feet. Before selecting the pods, allow them to dry. Seed pods will rupture if you don't pick them quickly enough.

**Lupine**

Lupine (Lupinus polyphyllus) is known for its stunning display of colors. These flowers are 1 to 4 foot long, stiff, with upright flower spikes that arise from horizontal foliage. These flowers resemble peas or sweet peas and are produced in big, densely packed racemes in deep blue, purple, yellow, pink, or white.

Lupines look great in borders, xeric (water-conserving) gardens, and scattered throughout native landscapes.

Lupine flowers bloom from early spring to the first weeks of July, depending on the variety and your zone. As a result, we recommend pairing them with some late-blooming summer favorites like zinnias, rudbeckias, and daisies to extend the season's vibrancy. Lupines are resistant to deer, and their blossoms attract pollinators such as bees, butterflies, and hummingbirds.

**Lupine Quick Guide: Planting, Growing, and Caring**

- ✓ Purple is the most popular color, but blue, yellow, pink, and white are all available.
- ✓ Cooler climates with average soil are preferred.
- ✓ Plant in direct, full sunlight to light shade; loosen the soil to allow for the growth of a long taproot
- ✓ Plant cold seeds in the springtime; otherwise, fall is the best time to plant seeds and plants
- ✓ Transplantation is not advised
- ✓ Early to mid-summer blooming

- ✓ Maturity: Blooming days vary depending on whether the plant is planted in the fall or spring; it blooms throughout July-August.
- ✓ Its height varies anywhere between 1 and 4 feet, depending on the variety.
- ✓ 12 inch spacing of flowers apart is recommended

**Preparing the Site**

Lupine is a simple to grow plant that thrives in chilly, damp environments. It enjoys full sun to light shade and medium soil, but it will grow in sandy, dry soil. Plants produce long taproots, so use a rototiller or a garden fork to loosen the soil to a depth of 12-20 inches. Clay is not conducive to their growth.

Lupine can be propagated through seeds, cuttings, or divisions. A 7-day cold treatment dramatically increases germination when growing from. Combine the seeds with wet paper towels in a sealed bag, such as Ziplock and store in the fridge. Another approach is soaking them for at least 24 hours in a slightly hot water. In the spring or summertime, seeds that have been treated can be placed in a seedbed until August 1st. The optimal time to plant untreated lupine seeds outside is between September and November.

Plants that are cultivated from seed will bloom the first year they are planted. To extend the flowering duration, pinch off "spent blossoms." To ensure healthy plants and abundant flowers, use an organic fertilizer once a month.

**Tip:** Plant lupines in masses in borders or scatter them throughout the cottage garden for dramatic results.

When growing from cuttings, a stem should be taken down to the trunk, including a little of its connected "footprint" to the trunk. Set in gritty sand or another propagation medium that is wet and well-drained. In the period of propagation, keep the plant covered except for a few minutes every day to air it out and enable it to acclimate.

To avoid disturbing the roots, start cuttings in larger pots that may be moved into the outdoors, pot and all.

Don't transplant directly since the long taproot is sensitive and could be harmed, which will cause the plant to fail.

**Insect and Disease Issues**

There aren't many pest concerns related to lupine. Aphids will infest plants occasionally. If pests are discovered, use the following common sense, non-toxic pest control method:

- ✓ Remove highly affected leaves or other plant components by pinching or pruning them
- ✓ Beneficial insects, such as ladybugs, are commercially available and are significant natural predators of the pest.
- ✓ For long-lasting protection, use organic Diatomaceous Earth (DE). DE works by scoring an insect's outer coat as it crawls over the fine powder. It contains no hazardous toxins.

- ✓ Safer® Soap is a short-acting natural pesticide that acts quickly on large infestations.
- ✓ Aphids prefer plants with a lot of nitrogen and fresh growth that is soft, so don't overfertilize.

**Instructions for Seed Saving**

Seed pods that are ripe erupt on their own. When the pods changes to yellow and the seeds inside begin to "rattle," they're ripe. Place them in a screen box to allow them rupture, then easily pick up the seed.

**California Poppy**

California poppies (Eschscholzia californica) are wispy, colorful flowers that conserve water while providing a beautiful display of long-lasting colors. Growing California poppies from seed reward home gardeners with wispy, fern-like leaves and vibrant orange, red, and yellow flowers. Despite its sunny California origins, this flower is a cool-season annual that grows to about 4-12 inches tall.

## California Poppy Quick Guide: Planting, Growing, and Caring

- ✓ It is a perennial that self-seeds readily in warm climates
- ✓ Direct-seed outdoors in fertile soil; direct, full sunlight is required
- ✓ Watering is minimal, and fertilizer is not used
- ✓ Blooms in the early summer through early autumn
- ✓ Harvest before the bloom opens to use as cut flowers
- ✓ From seed to flower, it takes 55-75 days
- ✓ Its height ranges from about 4-12 inches

- ✓ Space the flowers about 4-8 inches away in all directions

**Preparing the Site**

Enough sunshine, fertile, fast-draining soil, as well as plenty of water are all favorites of California poppies. They are, however, versatile and can withstand poor soil conditions and some dryness. Before planting, put a shovelful or two of well-aged compost or organic manure in the soil to enhance soil conditions and to promote abundant blooms.

**Planting Instructions**

Poppies dislike having their roots disturbed; thus, direct sowing is preferred. Sow early in the springtime, when the soil is still cool and mild frost is still a possibility. Seeding can also be done in the fall, just before the freezing of the ground. The seeds will germinate in 10-15 days. Poppy plants do not require a lot of water. Plants that receives lots of fertilizer will create large leaf growth at the price of blossom output. To extend the blossoming season, remove the "spent blossoms" or use them as cuttings in floral arrangements. Because poppies self-seed from year to year, make sure to leave some faded flowers on the plants, especially later in the year.

**Tip:** Snip stems and use a lighter or match to seal the end before putting them in an arrangement for long-lasting blossoms.

**Insect and Disease Issues**

There are a few pest issues when it comes to poppies. Aphids and thrips, on the other hand, can appear virtually overnight. Keep an eye out for these soft-bodied sucking insects and release ladybugs to help control the population. If the plants are heavily attacked, use an insecticidal soap containing pyrethrin. Gray mold, downy mildew, and powdery mildew are moisture-prone infections that can damage plants, and also affect foliage and blooms if left untreated. To decrease and avoid common plant diseases, use the following steps:

- ✓ If at all possible, avoid watering from above (use soaker hoses or drip irrigation)
- ✓ Plants should be properly spaced to facilitate air circulation
- ✓ To avoid additional infection, use organic fungicides

**Instructions for Seed Saving**

Seed savers will find it really simple. When the blossoms fade, a long, thin seedpod develops, which turns brown as it ages. Simply cut off the brown seedpod and leave it to dry completely before cracking apart and removing the hundreds of little sand-like seeds. Keep seeds in a chill and dry place.

# The end... almost!

Hey! We've made it to the final chapter of this book, and I hope you've enjoyed it so far.

If you have not done so yet, I would be incredibly thankful if you could take just a minute to leave a quick review on Amazon

Reviews are not easy to come by, and as an independent author with a little marketing budget, I rely on you, my readers, to leave a short review on Amazon.

Even if it is just a sentence or two!

So if you really enjoyed this book, please...

\>\> Click here to leave a brief review on Amazon.

I truly appreciate your effort to leave your review, as it truly makes a huge difference.

# Chapter 6

# Seed Saving Mistakes To Avoid

For the majority of my gardening career, I have depended on plants from my local nursery. I've done lots of seed saving, which appears straightforward, well, to me, but has certain drawbacks. Learn from my seed-saving mistakes before starting your seed-saving journey, some of which have already been discussed well enough in the pages of this book.

**Do not eat the herbs and vegetables grown for seed**: If you wish to save seeds from plants such as herbs or vegetables, you'll need one or two plants dedicated to the task. It's no longer safe to eat a herb like basil or a leafy food like lettuce once it blooms. Include a plant that will be allowed to bolt and produce blooms and seed heads.

**Hybrid seeds should not be saved:** The seeds produced by a hybrid plant will not produce the same results as the parent plant. A hybrid is a cross between two kinds that produces a third with distinct characteristics. The seeds from that hybrid have genetics that are unlikely to match the parent plant. Try it out for a laugh and see what you come up with, but it won't be the same as the original.

**Don't make things any more difficult than it needs to be:** Allowing plants to reseed is one of the simplest ways to reap the benefits of seeds already present in the garden. Harvesting seeds from your garden may be challenging with some plants, so if reseeding is the best option, let nature take its course. Some flowers self-seed, allowing you to grow fresh plants year after year with little effort. Put an end to late summer deadheading to enable seed heads to grow.

**Start with easy-to-grow seeds:** Flower seeds are easy to collect and store. Jusy allow the seed head to mature and dry before shaking free and storing the seeds. It can be a little more difficult when it comes to vegetables. Carrot seeds, for example, are tiny and difficult to come by. And there are plants which cross-pollinate, implying that the seeds, like hybrids, will not produce a true plant. Cucumber, melons, pepper, tomatoes, and beans are the easiest vegetables to start with since they have larger seeds and self-pollinate.

**Remember to dry the seeds:** Seeds must be completely dry before being stored. Simply leave the blossoms on the plant until they are totally dried. Beans are also simple to prepare. Pull the seeds from the pods after they have dried on the plant. Wet seeds, such as cucumbers and tomatoes, require an additional step. To ferment the seeds, soak them for some days inside water. This aids in the removal of pulpy particles. The good seeds will settle beneath (at the bottom) the container. Gather these, rinse them, and dry them before storing them. However, don't allow the seeds to be extremely dry because it would be difficult to have them reclaimed once it is over dried. Hence, it's important to perform some basic tests/ checks to know when a seed is dry enough before harvesting them for storage. Kindly revisit the "Drying The Seeds For Storage" section earlier discussed for more information.

**Don't start harvesting seeds too soon:** Seeds must be well mature to be planted in the following season. Flowers and seeds in pods should be left on the plant until they are fully mature and dry. Allow fruits such as tomatoes, melons, and cucumbers to ripe well enough before you harvest them.

**Failure to use cold storage when it is necessary:** If it's a seed that you intend to plant in a couple of months or a year, it'll be good at room temperature. However, if you wish to store those seeds for the future, you can refrigerate or freeze them. Seeds can live for several years if they are exposed to cold temperatures. Simply dry the seeds well enough before storing them in the fridge or in an airtight plastic or glass container.

And what happens when it's eventually time to take out these seeds?

When you take something from a cold environment and put it in a warmer environment, it condenses. When you take seeds out of the freezer, leave them out on the counter for four hours. This ensures that none of the humidity gets into the package, which, if they do, can damage the seeds.

**Seeds should be stored in direct sunlight:** For long-term seed viability, use a dry, dark location (think closets and cupboards).

Allowing seeds to be subjected to excessive temperature fluctuations: The heat from a sunny window and bursts of air conditioning can both alter the germination rates of stored seeds. Find the most steady temperature in your home; it may be a cellar or a closet—somewhere whose temperature is constant.

**Seeds are labeled incorrectly or not at all:** Keep the original seed package after pouring store-bought seeds into an airtight bottle. It's best to put the package inside the jar. That seed packet has a lot of useful information on it, so it's always a good idea to keep one on hand. Then, on the outside of the bottle, place an adhesive label. Always name the outside of the container and put a label on the inside of the container. This way, even if the outside label comes off, you'd still retain the inside label.

# Conclusion

The best – and cheapest – approach to propagate your garden is to save your seed. However, it is also a means of safeguarding our historical plants.

Seeds are saved for a variety of purposes by different people. Some do it to retain a legacy by planting a variety that their parents grew or one that is unique to their location. Some people do it to ensure a supply of seed from a variety that is no longer available. Some people save seed since it's something they've always done.

Whatever your reason for saving seeds, standard seed-saving procedures must be followed from start to finish to save the best seed variety successfully. This book has provided you with virtually all you need to get started in saving seeds successfully. So, ensure you thoroughly understand the points discussed in the pages of this book, and I sure hope you are able to get the best seed saved from your garden.

www.ingramcontent.com/pod-product-compliance
Lightning Source LLC
Chambersburg PA
CBHW071417070526
**44578CB00003B/593**